1914-1918

INTRODUCTION

The names of servicemen from Harefield who died during the First World War have been taken mainly from War Memorials. Harefield War Memorial is located on the village green. Harefield Church also has a memorial as does Bell's United Asbestos Company. While many lads from Harefield worked at Bell's, many came from the surrounding area and although they are included in this document, mainly no other details are given. In the main, not included are which war memorial the names are on, apart from where considered necessary or helpful. Uxbridge Local History Library possesses for reference most Rolls of Honour and names from the War Memorials. Many ex-soldiers suffered from their injuries for a long time after the end of hostilities. Some of their deaths may have been war-related but usually the men are not recorded on the war memorials. This is the case with George Hampstead who lived with his wife and children near the 'Spotted Dog' in Harefield. He had served with the Buffs for 2 years and 4 months and was for a considerable time, a Prisoner of War. He had received a blow on the head whilst a POW for refusing to work in a munitions factory since when he had suffered bad nose bleeds. His health had been gradually failing through neglect during the war, dysentery etc. He also was out of work. He passed away 'in the road' in about late January 1922.

Details from various Rolls of Honour have been matched with some of the men where confusion may exist as to why they are included in this document or where there are conflicting details. This matching maybe erroneous, but in some instances this has proved to be too difficult, particularly in cases where names or initials are similar or where the serviceman was known by a nickname.

Other details are provided, where known, and come from a variety of sources - the Commonwealth War Graves Commission registers; *The Great War: the standard history of the all-Europe conflict*; *de Ruvigny's Roll of Honour*; local papers; *The Times*; various regimental histories, archive material from Uxbridge Local Studies Library and Monumental Inscriptions from various churches and graveyards. Some of the details from the sources not only differ in the amount of information provided, but also occasionally conflict. Further, not all soldiers who died in this war are listed in the volumes of Soldiers Died..., and the Commonwealth War Graves Commission apart from not having had in some instances any details from relatives of the deceased, do also have problems locating names where no service number is available, especially in the case of common names. Not many details have been found in most cases where the servicemen born in this locality had moved to other areas.

Maps to show where the serviceman died are given in some instances and the regimental crests are also provided in other instances.

Please note that where a serviceman's record exists on the 'Ancestry' site, these details are not included here. Also that regimental diaries do not usually mention the names of ordinary ranks when they are killed in action or wounded and sometimes, not even the officers are mentioned. War diaries vary from the informative to the boring.

For the purposes of the Commonwealth War Graves Commission the dates of World War One are 4th August 1914 – 31st August 1921 and the official date of the end of the First World War is 31st August 1921.

Places of burial as recorded in local papers ('buried.....') can differ from where the deceased was eventually buried or commemorated as many burials were later disturbed by heavy fire.

Servicemen posted as missing in action were not declared officially killed until up to one year had passed and a military tribunal heard the facts relating to the disappearance. If the loss of records meant that a date could not officially be declared, then an arbitrary date was decided upon. A notification of 'missing in action' meant an immediate loss of income and the uncertainty of any pension rights, which was so devastating to a married man.

Every reasonable care had been taken in compiling this document. Responsibility cannot be accepted for any errors or omissions.

Information regarding the graves of other British Service Personnel can be obtained from the Ministry of Defence.

My thanks are extended to the Local History Library staff at Uxbridge Library for their co-operation, Stephen Britton, Eric Button and Joss Martin. The Commonwealth War Graves Commission has also to be thanked for their help in the early years before their website existed.

ALLEN, Herbert William

Born at Stilton, Hunts., on 8th September 1898,

enlisted at Harrow in February 1916. 45425, Private, 18th Lancashire Fusiliers. He had been reported missing in the Ypres Salient on October 22nd 1917, but it is presumed that he was killed on or about that date, aged 19. On that date the 35th Division on the north of the line at the Third Battle of Ypres was in operations in cooperation with the French near Poelcappelle. The Lancashire Fusiliers, despite a magnificent battle, were unable to maintain their most advanced positions. German shell-fire and especially the enemy snipers from the wood on the left and from the covered road, were the cause of heavy losses. Son of Mr. and Mrs. Henry Allen of Park Lane, Harefield. His father was a policeman in the Metropolitan Police Force. Herbert was educated for a short time at Harefield School, which he joined from Harrow Road School on 3rd September 1906. Before enlisting he had been employed at the West Hyde Joinery Works. He is commemorated on Harefield War Memorial and a Herbert Allen is also commemorated on the Bell's United Asbestos War Memorial. Commemorated: Tyne Cot Memorial, Zonnebeke, West Vlaanderen, Belgium.

BATES, W.

He is commemorated on the Bell's United Asbestos War Memorial. W. Bates is recorded on the SSFA document which records all the men from Harefield who enlisted prior to early 1916. Possibly William Bates who was born at Amersham, enlisted at Bedford into the 7th Bedfordshire Regiment and who lived at Watford. He died on 14th May 1918, probably as a POW, and is buried at Hautmont Communal Cemetery, Nord, France.

BELL, J.
He is commemorated on the Church Memorial and on the war memorial on the village green. There is also a J.W. Bell commemorated on the Bell's Asbestos Company's Memorial, but as there is no such name on the Soldiers' and Sailors' Families Association record, he would have enlisted in the Army or Navy after about the spring of 1916.

BLAKE, A.W.
He is commemorated on the Bell's United Asbestos War Memorial. Possibly Arthur Blake of Aldenham, Herts. He was serving in the 8th East Surrey Regiment and was killed in action on 12th August 1916 and is commemorated on the Ploegsteert Memorial in Belgium. The 18th Division, who had been in action at Deville Wood in desperate fighting in July and had spent August in a comparatively quiet part of the line at Armentieres.

BRANCH, Harry
Born on 1st September 1888 and baptized at Harefield on 28th October the same year, son of Charles and Emma Branch, nee Bugbee, enlisted at Harrow, lived at Weymouth Cottage, Walton-on-Thames. 6786, Private, 6th Northumberland Fusiliers, formerly

G/25170, Middlesex Regiment. Second son of Mr.

Charles Branch of 1 Rosemary Lane, Harefield. He had been wounded on the Somme in the latter stages of the battle and on November 22nd 1916 his parents were informed that their son was in No. 10 RAMC General Hospital, Rouen, suffering from gunshot wounds to his feet. He was transferred to Birmingham Civil General Hospital where he died of shrapnel wounds to his chest and a lung abscess on 26th December 1916, aged 28. He is commemorated on both Harefield War Memorial and on the Church Memorial. Buried: Birmingham (Lodge Hill) Cemetery.

BRAUNTON, H.

He is commemorated on the Bell's United Asbestos War Memorial and on the memorial at St. Mary's, Rickmansworth as W.H. Braunton, which is correct. William Henry Braunton was born in about 1891 in Bideford in Devon and was a labourer when he enlisted at Watford, serving in 'X' 1st Trench Mortar Battery, Royal Field Artillery. He was killed in action on 16th April 1916 and buried at St. Patrick's Cemetery at Loos. He had married Mary Anne Elizabeth Tibbles in late 1908 and was the son-in-law of Mrs. M. Tibbles of Rickmansworth, who lost at least three relations in the First World War and one in the Second World War.

BREWER, W.

He is commemorated on Harefield War Memorial and on the Memorial at St. Mary's Church. Probably Walter or William Brewer, below.

BREWER, Walter Edwin

Born in about 1883 at Portsea. Able Seaman, 202903. HMS/M. "E.13" (HMS Dolphin). Royal Navy. He had been in the Navy for a number of years when he died of heart failure on 26th March 1920, aged 36. Son of Thomas and Elizabeth Brewer of Portsmouth; husband of Ada Brewer (nee Schey) of High Street, Harefield. They had married locally early in 1914. He was one of the crew of the submarine which had been stranded while being shelled 'somewhere in the North Sea' (the Danish belt) in August 1915 and was one of the few to be saved and interned. He was unwounded despite the Germans firing on the crew. He was allowed home in early 1918 for about one month after which he had to return to be reinterned. He is commemorated by the CWGC. Buried: Harefield (St. Mary) Churchyard.

BREWER, William

Born at Harefield on 21st June 1894, enlisted at Hounslow in September 1914, of Pinner Road, Harefield. 19437, Private,  2nd Suffolk Regiment. On 3rd September 1915, the Regiment had been employed in pioneer work between Moat Farm and Hooge and on 23rd September 1915, the Battalion had moved to Maple Copse, near where he was killed in action on the opening day of the Battle of Loos, against the 248 and 246 Reserve Infantry Regiments of the 54th Reserve Division of Wurtembergers on 25th September 1915, in an attack from Railway Wood to

Sanctuary Wood, aged 21. An exploding shell had hit him as he was passing the firing line with ammunition and bombs. This action became known as the second attack on Bellewaarde and was part of a subsidiary operation to distract the enemy. He had joined the 18th Hussars (25425) in September 1914, subsequently transferring to the Suffolk Regiment. He was educated at Harefield School, joining it from the infant school on 2nd June 1902, and had worked at Messrs. Sainsbury's at Southall. He is commemorated on the Wesleyan Chapel. Son of Walter of the same address. Commemorated: Ypres (Menin Gate) Memorial, Belgium.

BROWN, George Thomas, DCM

Born at Harefield on February 10th 1886 and baptized

there on 30th May that same year, enlisted Uxbridge, of 28 Oxford Cottage, Iver. 20651, Sergeant, 17th Coy., Machine Gun Corps (Infantry). Formerly 7811, 1st North Staffs Regt. During the whole month of July 1917 the British Army knew an attack was pending. All roads north of Armentieres were thick with troops moving up day after day. Our front was at that time about eleven miles long round the Ypres salient and north of Ypres it was around the Yser Canal. On 29th July thunderstorms made the ground very wet which filled shell-holes with water and hampered all movements. He was killed in action in battle at the Battle of the Ridges, part of the Third Battle of Ypres, on 31st July 1917, the day the Ypres great ill-fated offensive was opened on a front of 15miles from La Bassee Ville on the River Lys to Steenstraate on the Yser Canal, the main object being an arc of small hills in front of the British valley positions around Ypres. Zero hour was 3.50am. Twelve divisions advanced on an eleven-mile front in pouring rain. He was aged 33, the son of William and Elizabeth Rachel Brown of Hill End, Harefield; husband of Nellie Brown, nee Green, whom he had married by special license at Iver parish church a few weeks before he was killed. He had been a reservist and was posthumously awarded the Distinguished Conduct Medal for conspicuous bravery at Hill 60 at Messines Ridge while serving with the MGC. Hill 60 had been taken from the French in December 1914. It was of considerable tactical importance, since from its summit the enemy were able to observe the British movements. He was educated at Harefield School which he joined from the infants' on 29th July 1893. He is commemorated on the village green and Church memorials. Commemorated: Ypres (Menin Gate) Memorial, Belgium.

CARTER, H.

 He is commemorated on the Bell's United Asbestos War Memorial. Henry William Carter lived at West Hyde and served with the 2nd Royal Fusiliers. The Battalion had landed in Gallipoli on 25th April 1915. Off X beach HMS *'Implacable'* and HMS *'Swiftsure'* in support as they landed under cover of a terrible bombardment. A series of delays gave the fully warned Turks 5 weeks to prepare. On 24th June 1915 the French attacked a system of trenches on the slopes of Kerevez Dere. They met with intense fire and suffered heavy losses and did not reach their objective. A similar movement, on its left, gave the

British a progression of 700 yards of Gully Ravine. He was killed in action on 28th June 1915 in Gallipoli at the Battle of Gully Ravine as the Fusiliers advanced beyond the high ground above the sea under heavy artillery and rifle fire – which forever afterwards became known as Fusilier Bluff. Turks had been spotted massing at the east end of their objective (J12 and J13 trenches). By 15.40 the 2nd Royal Fusiliers, in desperate need of bombs and water, held half on J13 and the Turks held the other half and reports were received that the enemy were massing in both trenches. The Munster Fusiliers and later the Gurkhas were set in to clear the trenches of the Germans. At 6am on the following morning the 2nd Royal Fusiliers were relieved. He is commemorated on the Helles Memorial.

CHRISTOPHER, G. C.
He is commemorated on the Bell's United Asbestos War Memorial.

CLARE, Charles Sidney
Born at Stratford, Essex, enlisted London, lived at Harefield. 13753, Lance-Corporal, 1st Scots Guards. He is recorded as killed on 10th October 1917 a quiet day and a day spent resting. However, the 1st Scots Guards had been in action on the previous day north of the main attack at Ypres which is more likely the date upon Lance Corporal Clare was killed. On the evening of 7th October 1917, the 1st and 2nd Guards Brigade went into their respective sectors on the front and was ready in their assembly positions by 1am near the Broembeek, close to where he was killed in action in a failed enemy counter-attack during the Third Battle of Ypres. There had been a counter-

attack in the afternoon from the south-western corner of the Houthulst Forest against the Faidherbe crossroads. It had been pouring with rain all day and the deep artillery and machine-gun barrage was intense and accurate. The operations had been aided by the Australians and the French First Army. Commemorated: Tyne Cot Memorial, Zonnebeke, West Vlaanderen, Belgium.

CLARE, Sidney
Born in Leytonstone in about 1894, son of Esther Clare. He is commemorated on the Bell's United Asbestos War Memorial and on the Church Memorial. Probably a mistake for Charles Sidney Clare, above.

CLARK, Joseph
Born at Harefield on 8th September 1893, enlisted at Harefield on 14th July 1911, lived at 'Rossland', Harefield. TF/1377, Private, 8th Middlesex Regiment. He had at first been reported as missing near Politze at the battle of St. Julian during the Second Battle of Ypres which took place between 24th April and 4th May 1915, during which gas had been used and later accounted for, but died in one of the several Casualty Clearing Stations at Bailleul on 26th May 1915 of gas poisoning received near Politze during terrible fighting, aged 22. Son of James and Sarah Clark of 'Rossland', Park Terrace, Uxbridge. He was educated at schools in Harefield after which he had been apprenticed to Mr. Charles Brown, a carpenter, and was an enthusiastic cricketer. He is commemorated on St. Mary's Memorial. Buried: Bailleul Communal Cemetery Extension, Nord, France, F.113.

CLEWLEY, Thomas Albert

Born Blackfriars, London, enlisted London, lived at Harefield. 51226, Private, 'C' Coy, X1 Platoon, 4th Liverpool Regiment. Formerly 46716, Northumberland Regiment. The 33rd Division had arrived on the scene of action (the Battle of the Lys) on April 11th 1918, and had come into line on 13th April and on 16th, the 4th Liverpools were west of Meteren. The Division had been detailed to cover Meteren to the west of Bailleul against a northward sweep of the Germans. It was at once thrust in to fill the gap in front of Bailleul, where it found itself involved from 13th April onwards in most desperate fighting. Germans, advancing, without a bombardment, drove in the left flank on Meteren, annihilating the left company thus forcing them to retire on Meteren. On the following day their front extended from the back of Meteren to behind Bailleul with the 4th King's Liverpools, 32nd and 116th Chasseurs a Pied, 1st Middlesex, 2nd Argylls and 5th Tank Battalion Lewis guns in the line. At 9am the Germans released a very heavy artillery bombardment. Half an hour later Germans of the 81st Reserve and 38th Divisions were seen moving in column among the hedges close by. At 6pm, after a short bombardment, the Germans advanced against the whole front held by the 98th Brigade, severely attacking the 4th Liverpools, captured a farm in the front line on the Meteren-Fletre road, but immediately driven out by a counter-attack in which portions of the 4th Liverpools, 1st Middlesex and newly arrived units of the French 133rd Division took part. Sometime on this day, he went missing, believed killed in action on 17th April 1918, aged 19. On that day, eight German divisions had attacked

Kemmel. Son of Thomas, who had died on 17th December 1917, aged 46 and is buried at Harefield, and Rose Flora Clewley of "Columba House", Harefield, who died after a painful illness at the end of 1924. His sister, Rose, died on 22nd November 1920, aged 23. He is commemorated on the village green and Church memorials. Commemorated: Tyne Cot Memorial, Zonnebeke, West Vlaanderen, Belgium.

COLLETT, A.
He is commemorated on the Harefield War Memorial and the Church Memorial. Probably a mistake for Thomas Collett below.

COLLETT, George
Private. Son of Mr. and Mrs. Collett of High Street, Harefield. Reported to have died in action on Easter Sunday 1918 (31st March 1918). He had had his 19th birthday two weeks before he was killed. He had been formerly employed at the Asbestos Works.

COLLETT, Thomas Alfred
Born Hull (Willamton, Yorks), enlisted at Harrow early in the war, lived at Harefield. G/71552, Private, 23rd Royal Fusiliers. Formerly TR/10/25758 TR Battalion. On the afternoon of March 12th 1918, the Battalion was in the trenches again at Lincoln Reserve and Midland Reserve, with 'D' Company in Snap Trench. On that night and for the next two nights, the Battalion suffered heavy casualties from a gas bombardment. Then they were relieved by New Zealand troops and marched back to the wood at Mailly-Maillet and then to Equancourt for rest and for all to recover from gas poisoning. Next came the

German spring offensive on the Somme on 21st March. On 23rd bullets rained down on the 23rd RF camp. Every man turned out and took up a line north of Equancourt in an attempt to hold up the enemy's advance after the fall of Fins but had not enough men for the purpose. On the following morning an enemy attack was beaten back with heavy loss. In the following days, they were heavily attacked and on relief the Battalion marched out of Mailly-Maillet for a rest at Englebelmer, with only four officers and 70 men. During 1st -3rd April 1918, there was a lull in the fighting, although here and there around Englebelmer some vicious skirmishes took place. He was killed in action here on 1st April 1918, aged 19. Son of Isaac and Mary Collett of 6 Waterloo Cottages, Harefield. Buried: Mesnil Communal Cemetery, Somme, France, C.17.

COLLIER, Frederick

He is commemorated on the Bell's United Asbestos War Memorial.

Probably Frederick Herbert Collier who was born at West Hyde, Herts., enlisted and lived at Uxbridge. 3481, Lance-Corporal, 8th Royal Fusiliers (City of London Regiment). Killed in action in France by a shell explosion at 10.30am on 11th April 1916, aged 20. They were relieving the 7th Sussex Regiment in front line trenches at 9am and at 10.30am just as the relief had been completed the enemy exploded a mine. He was with his friend Cpl. F. Batchelor 'of Uxbridge' at the time who was also killed. In 1916 mining operations had been rigorously continued and mines had been blown by the enemy in the Quarries sector on 24th March in reply to one we had blown on 19th. Again mines were exploded by us on 26th, 27th

March, 5th, 13th, 20th, 21st and 22nd April – and by the enemy in retaliation on 31st March, 2nd, 8th, 11th, 12th and 23rd April. Although no action on a big scale ensued, theses explosions entailed fighting and consolidation, leading to casualties. Son of James and Alice Collier of 1 Fishery Cottages, Harefield. Buried: Vermelles British Cemetery, Pas de Calais, France, L.25.

COMPTON, H.

 He is commemorated on the Bell's United Asbestos War Memorial and on the memorial at St. Mary's, Rickmansworth. He was serving as a Lance Corporal in the West Riding Regiment and died on 20th April 1918 and buried at Rickmansworth (Chorleywood Road) Cemetery.

COOPER, John William
Born Harefield, lived and enlisted at Harefield in September 1916. G/52107, Private, 10th Royal Fusiliers. Formerly TR/10/53586, 102nd T.R. Battn. From 18th until 27th September 1917 the 10th Royal Fusiliers were at Wakefield Huts but returned to the line north of the Ypres-Comines Canal. On 29th September, the 11th Brigade of the 37th Division had been sent up at once to near the Menin Road to help the survivors of an attack to form a connected line, where he was killed in action at the battle of Polygon Wood in a violent counter-attack on 29th September 1917, aged 19 (20). Because of the state of the ground, many men drowned in the shell holes. He had previously been wounded. Son of Mr. and Mrs. Edward Cooper of Nelson's Yard, Harefield and

brother of Mr. F. Cooper of 22 Vernon Drive, Harefield. He had been educated at Harefield Schools and is commemorated on both of Harefield's War Memorial (village green and St. Mary's Church). Buried: Perth Cemetery (China Wall), Zillebeke, Ieper, Belgium.

COOPER, Thomas

 All that is known is that he was of Harefield and had for some time been employed as first footman by Commander and Mrs. Tarleton of Breakspears, Harefield. He was serving with the 4th Royal Fusiliers and after seeing a great deal of heavy fighting was killed in action or died of wounds sometime around October 1917. He is commemorated on Harefield War Memorial, on the Church Memorial and on the Breakspear Memorial. No other details are known.

CULLEN, Thomas

He lived at Breakspeare Road, Harefield. Petty Officer 1st Class, 127044, RN. HMS '*Victory*'. 'Died of illness contracted from exposure in the North Sea Patrol on 27th November 1916' at Queensferry Hospital. He was 49 and unmarried and had been a head chauffeur for Commander Tarleton of Breakspear for a number of years. He was probably a reservist as he was called out for service when the Navy mobilized on 2nd August, 1914. He is commemorated on Harefield War Memorial and on the Breakspear Estate Memorial. Buried: Dalmeny and Queensferry Cemetery, West Lothian.

DOUGLAS, William Henry

Born at Harefield, son of George and Jane Douglas. He was a casual labourer and enlisted in London in the 3rd Depot RFA as Gunner on 4th January 1913 and joined at Preston on 6th January. He was posted Gunner 54th RFA on 5th March 1913 and 101st RFA on 20th January 1914. 71243, Gunner, 101st Bty., Royal Field Artillery. He died at the Station Hospital at Quetta from bronchopneumonia at 6.45am on 3rd October 1918. At the end of 1914 he had been taken ill with malaria. Son of Mr. and Mrs. Douglas of Hill End, Harefield. He is commemorated on the Church Memorial. Ernest Douglas, who lived at Rickmansworth who died on 22nd March 1918 while serving with the Hertfordshire Regiment was probably his cousin. Ernest is not commemorated on the memorial at St. Mary's Church at Rickmansworth. William is buried in Quetta Government Cemetery, India; Commemorated: Delhi Memorial (India Gate).

DRURY, T.

He is commemorated on the Bell's United Asbestos War Memorial.

DUKE, H.

He is commemorated on the Church Memorial. As he is not recorded on the Soldiers' and Sailors' Families Association (Harefield) document, he will have enlisted after the spring of 1916 or maybe lived just outside Harefield but worshipped at St. Mary's Church. .

EVANS, Leonard
'Son of William of 5, Belle Vue Terrace, Harefield. Royal Field Artillery. His father had served during the Afghanistan campaign'. SEE FOSTER, Leonard

EVANS, Thomas Henry
Born Portslade-by-Sea, Sussex. Able Seaman 197379 (RFR PO B/5622). Died when the battleship '*Bulwark*' blew up accidentally whilst lying in Rithole Reach, at Sheerness on November 26th, 1914, aged 30. The only definite conclusion made by the Admiralty Court of Enquiry was that the ignition which has taken place was internal and not external. Son of the late Thomas William and Isabella Evans of Hawthorn Cottage, Harefield; husband of Louise Evans of 5 Bellevue Terrace, Harefield. He had been in the navy for 14 years and had served in the Somaliland campaign and received a medal. He was a Reservist working at the Asbestos Works and had already served on HMS '*Prince of Wales*' at some time. He left a wife and 4 year old child. A younger daughter, Doris Evelyn Evans, had died in October 1913, aged 5 weeks. He is commemorated on the Bell's United Asbestos War Memorial as well as on Harefield War Memorial and St. Mary's Church Memorial. Buried: Harefield (St. Mary) Churchyard.

EVANS, William
Born Notting Hill, enlisted at Harefield where he lived as is commemorated on the War Memorial and the memorial in St. Mary's Church. G/20126, Private, 1st Middlesex Regiment. Died of wounds, probably in either the 34th or 2/2nd London CCS at Meaulte or Grovetown which had been set up to deal with casualties wounded in the later stages of the Battle of

the Somme battlefield, on 4th November 1916, aged 38. He may have been wounded on 28th October in the attack and capture of Rainy and Dewdrop Trenches, or at the Flers line the following day. On 1st November they were in the front line at Stormy Trench. Buried: Grove Town Cemetery, Meaulte, Somme, France.

FIELD, W.
He is commemorated on the Bell's United Asbestos War Memorial.

FOSTER, Leonard

Born New Malden, enlisted Kingston-on-Thames at the commencement of hostilities. 95702, Gunner, Royal Field Artillery, 'A' Battery, 93rd Army Brigade. Killed in action near Neuville Vitasse on the first day of the Battle of Arras, on Easter Monday, 9th April 1917, aged 25. At 5.30am the British forces attacked on a front of 40km from Arras to Lens and Havrincourt wood on the banks of the Ancre and had great success north of Arras. Son of Mrs. Charlotte Evans (formerly Foster) of 5 Belle Vue Terrace, Harefield, later of Rickmansworth, and the late Samuel Foster. He is neither commemorated on Harefield War Memorial nor on the St. Mary's Church Memorial at Rickmansworth. The map shows the trenches at Arras around the time Len was killed. Buried: La Targette British Cemetery, Neuville-St. Vaast, Pas de Calais.

FREESTONE, (C.J.) George

 Born at Harefield on 25th December 1893 and resided at High Street, Harefield, enlisted at Harrow in March 1917. P.W. 4825, Private, Middlesex Regiment, 19th (2nd Public Works) Battalion. He was wounded on 21st October 1917 at the Third Battle of Ypres. His wound was dressed by Private Thomas Ryder who carried the wounded man to a dressing station. He died of wounds to the leg and arm at a Casualty Clearing Station (the 34th or 36th) on 22nd October 1917. Son of Mr. and Mrs. G. Freestone of 7 Waterloo Cottages, Harefield. He was educated at Harefield schools and had worked for Messrs. Coles Shadbolt Cement Works. He is commemorated on both the Harefield War Memorial and St. Mary's Church Memorial as G. Freestone. Buried: Zuydcoote Military Cemetery, Nord, France.

FRENCH, Charles Herbert

Born and lived at Harefield, enlisted at Uxbridge on 25th August 1914. 16262, Private, 24th Royal Fusiliers (City of London Regiment). The war diary shows that he had been wounded sometime in November 1916, although no date is given. He died of these wounds on 16th November 1916. He may have been injured in the front line on 12th November or on 13th November in an attack on the German lines between Serre and Beaumont Hamel. Several men were wounded on this day from our own barrage. There were several Casualty Clearing Stations at Warlencourt, he may have died in one of these. Son of Henry and Lottie French. Buried: Warlincourt

Halte British Cemetery, Saulty, Pas de Calais, France.

FRENCH, H.
He is commemorated on Harefield War Memorial and the Church Memorial. Most probably a mistake for Charles Herbert French

GLIDEWELL, Percy
Born on 23rd December 1889, son of Minnie and Thomas Glidewell, enlisted at Putney, lived at Uxbridge. 2331, Private, City of London Yeomanry (Rough Riders). The capture of Ismail Oglu Tepe, a hill which rose 350 feet, was considered an essential preliminary to the seizure of the Anafarta heights. On 21st August 1915, as they were advancing from the direction of Chocolate Hill that afternoon over a hill or a plain about 2 or 3 miles wide which they were crossing in extended order, the scheme went horribly wrong. In fact, the operations at Suvla Bay on that date failed completely at every point, as a terrible, steady and accurate hail of shrapnel from the Turkish batteries, caused the heaviest losses. He was killed in 'the yeomanry charge' in action on this day at the Battle of Scimitar Hill (Hill 70) and the attack on Hill 60. Son of Thomas Glidewell of Watts Common, Harefield. His mother died suddenly from heart failure following bronchitis, on 3rd January 1919, aged 62; his father on 27th January 1921. Percy was educated at Harefield School which he joined from the infants' on 1st June 1898. He had worked as a kennelman to Mr. Stedall, junior, of Harefield but prior to his enlistment he was in the service of Lord Salisbury. He is commemorated on both the Harefield

War Memorial and on the Church Memorial. Buried: Green Hill Cemetery, Turkey.

GOMM, H.

He is commemorated on the Bell's United Asbestos War Memorial.

Probably Harry Gomm who was born at West Hyde, enlisted at Uxbridge and lived at West Hyde. He was serving as a Lance-Corporal with the 9th Royal Fusiliers. On 1st July 1916, they had moved up to Nab trenches near La Boiselle from billets at Frechencourt in support. He was killed in action in a series of local operations on the following day and is commemorated on the Thiepval Memorial on the Somme. They had taken over trenches from what was left of the 70th Brigade which had been decimated by machine-gun fire the previous day. The 2nd July was a fairly quiet day but a bombardment continued. A Harry Gomm, born on 9th October 1889, son of Emmanuel Gomm, was educated at Harefield School, which he joined from the infants' on 1st June 1898.

GRAY, Frederick

 Born Marylebone, enlisted at Harrow, lived with his parents at Park Lane, Harefield. 44812, Private, 'D' Coy., X111 Platoon, 7th Lincolnshire Regiment. The night of 21st-22nd March 1918 was relatively quiet except for the shelling of the Flesquieres Salient. Fred was reported missing since 23rd March 1918, in action here in the Salient, three weeks after arriving in France, aged 19. At 9.30am on 22nd a strong attack, the first serious fighting of the day, was launched against Hermies, garrisoned by the 7th Lincs, and which the Germans were determined to take. For eight hours they had fought magnificently in defense of the village. By dusk, the enemy had abandoned the assault. On the following day the battalion was to go into reserve at 1 o'clock behind the southern sector of the 'Red Line', two miles in the rear, ready if necessary to spread out on that line, which was not yet dug. No serious attack was made on them during that time. Later that day whilst holding Hermies they were almost cut off by the 51st Brigade, forcing them southwards towards the Canal du Nord. Working westwards they eventually reached Bertincourt. Elated at the capture of Hermies, the enemy columns advanced in close formation down the Hermies-Bertincourt road. By evening the 17th Division was in its appointed place in reserve, near Rocquigny. Son of Mr. and Mrs. Gray of Blenheim Cottage, Harefield. Prior to enlisting he had worked at the Asbestos Works and later was a gardener at Harefield Grove. He is commemorated on both the Harefield War Memorial and on the Church Memorial. Commemorated: Arras Memorial, Pas de Calais, France.

HALE, George Garibaldi
Born Brixton, enlisted Chichester, and resided at Harefield, although he is not commemorated on any local memorial. L/10236, Private, 1st Royal West Surrey Regiment. The 1st Queens had landed at Le Havre on 13th August 1914. After action on the Aisne they travelled by rail to Flanders and Belgium in flat countryside extending between Bethune and Ypres. Their goal was to help the Belgians hold territory around the Yser river and to stop the German offensive on Dunkerque and Calais and then close in

on Antwerp. The enemy aim was the secure positions in ports along the English Channel and North Sea to tighten their noose around France, which would also provide ideal submarine and warship bases. It would also greatly hamper the movement of troops from across the Channel. He was killed in action at Verneuil in spasmodic shelling all through the day during the 'Race to the Sea', which had begun on 18th September, on 7th October 1914. The 1st Queen's had suffered the most during the siege of Mons. On 7th October they were sent off to act as flank guards on the Schelde and then on to Durme as the Germans closed in on Antwerp. Two enemy battalions of the 37th Landwehr Brigade had already succeeded in crossing the Schelde at Schoonaerde on that morning. He was serving with the Expeditionary Force. Son of John and Clara Hale of Brixton. He had been a casual labourer and had joined the Sussex Regiment in London on 6th May 1912. Commemorated: La Ferte-sous-Jouarre Memorial, Seine-et-Marne, France.

HARDY, Arthur James

Born at Norwood on 12th May 1892 and baptized at

Southall in June 1892, son of Thomas and Jane, enlisted at Southall. 43858, Lance-Corporal, 17th Middlesex Regiment. Died of wounds on 3rd February 1918, aged 25. The 17th Middlesex Regiment was disbanded on 22nd February 1918. One of their last big battles was on 3rd January. They had been in reserve and moved during the night of 2nd-3rd January into the front line on the right bank of the Canal du Nord. At 4.20am on the morning of 3rd January the enemy advanced prior to which there was a hostile bombardment. A large number of Germans were dressed in white and could hardly be seen in the snow attacking solidly, killing 8, wounding 21, possibly Lance-Corporal Hardy was one of them, and 16 were missing. Son of Mr. and Mrs. Thomas Hardy of Southall; husband of Alice Hardy, nee Peverill, of Park Lane, Harefield, whom he had married on 14th April 1914. She was probably the sister of John Peverill, below. Two of Arthur's brothers, William and Harry were killed in action or died of wounds or illness and a fourth brother, George, died in 1932 after falling from a ladder. The fall was attributed to damage done to his feet by Trench Foot contracted while on service. Arthur had been educated at Featherstone Road School at Southall. He is commemorated on the memorial at Harefield. Buried: Rocquigny-Equancourt Road British Cemetery, Somme, France, A.3.

HARLAND, Reginald Wickham

Born at Harefield Vicarage on 10th November 1883 and baptized there on 11th December the same year. Captain, 1st (or 2nd) Battalion Hampshire Regiment. As the Germans were trying to break through to Dunkirk and Ypres, he was killed in action at Ploegsteert during heavy fighting when a bullet struck him in the head whilst watching the field with his glasses to sight the enemy on 30th October 1914, aged almost 32. Shortly before his death Captain Harland was ordered to drive the Germans out of a French town and they readily set about the attack. One of them was so badly wounded that he begged Captain Harland to draw his revolver and shoot him. Instead he bound up his comrade's wounds as well as he could and successfully conveyed him from the fighting line to a place of safety. Seventh of the nine sons of the Revd. Albert Augustus Harland, Vicar of Harefield, and Mrs. Louisa Ellen Harland of The Lodge, Harefield. The Rev. A.A. Harland was Vicar of the parish of Harefield for 50 years and had also been a member of the Parish Council. He was born in Yorkshire, the fourth son of Dr. Harland, thrice mayor of Scarborough. He married Louisa Wilson in 1865 and in the same year became curate of Ruislip. At Christmas 1870 he was offered the incumbency of Harefield, which he held until 1920 and died on 21st December 1921, aged 82, and is buried at Harefield. Capt. Harland was educated at Temple Grove School, East Sheen, Wellington College and Sandhurst. He was gazetted 2nd Lieut. in the Hampshire Regt. on 22nd April 1903, and promoted Lieut. 22nd December 1905 and Captain 9th August 1911. One of his brothers, the fourth son of his parents, Lieutenant Edwin Harland, Hampshire Regiment, commanding 'C' Squadron Rhodesian Regiment after the Captain had been wounded, was killed by a bullet in the South African war on the eve of the Relief of Mafeking, while trying to save the life of another officer. He had joined the Army in about 1892 and received his lieutenant's commission on 21st June 1894 and had displayed such talent, both as a soldier and a scout, he was called 'Baden Powell the Second'. Edwin had distinguished himself in the Matabele War and had been awarded a medal in 1894. Two other brothers were both wounded in the Dardanelles in 1915. His sister, Margaret, had died at Meerut from enteric in 1905. He is not commemorated locally. His father told the local press that 'he died as he had wished, for the sake of his

King and country'. Buried: Ploegsteert Churchyard, Belgium, A.3.

HARMAN, John

Born at Harefield on 2nd March 1889, enlisted Mill Hill. P.W. 6278, Private, 16th Middlesex Regiment (Public Schools) Battalion. Died of wounds in hospital at Etaples on 26th April 1917, aged 28. He may have been wounded on 14th April 1917 at Orange Hill or between 15th and 18th April when they were engaged in making new defenses at Monchy where 59 were wounded or he may have been wounded sometime after 23rd April at Monchy-le-Preux in action with the 3rd Bavarians. Son of John and Ellen Elizabeth Harman of 8 Waterloo Villas, Harefield. He was educated at Harefield School, joining from the infants on 1st June 1897. He is commemorated on St. Mary's Church Memorial only. Buried: Etaples Military Cemetery, Pas de Calais, France.

HEARD, Joseph Henry

Born Enfield, enlisted Uxbridge, and resided at Harefield. G/43724, Private, 1/7th Middlesex Regiment. The 56th Division had fought its way to the Hindenburg Line on 23rd August 1918. Their immediate task was to hem in and capture Croiselles. At 3am on 26th August 1918 when advancing to Fooly Trench and Croisilles Reserve Trench, they were met by a hail of machine-gun and rifle fire. From the high ground north-west of Croisilles the fire was particularly deadly. He was killed in this action on this date, aged 26. Son of Joseph H. and Emma Heard; husband of Ellen K. Heard of "Isca", 28 Hillingdon Road, Uxbridge. He had worked on the

Breakspeare estate. He had joined the 2/8th Middlesex

on 11th September 1914, going to Gibraltar on 1st February 1915 and transferred to Egypt in August. There he fought the Turks. He returned to France early in the spring of 1916 and took part in the battle of the Somme and in all subsequent engagements. Whilst on leave in December 1916 he had married Ellen Wassell. He is commemorated on the Breakspear Estate Memorial and Harefield War Memorial and on St. Mary's Memorial. The map shows The Battles of Albert and the Scarpe 1918. Commemorated: Vis-en-Artois Memorial, Pas de Calais, France.

HENSBY, F. (or E.)
He is commemorated on the Bell's United Asbestos War Memorial.

HILTON, E.
He is commemorated on Harefield War Memorial and on St. Mary's Church Memorial
Probably a mistake for (Second) Lieutenant Henry Denne Hilton, 5th Middlesex Regiment attd. 4th Battalion. He lived at the Red House, Harefield. On the evening of 14th December 1914, the 4th Middlesex took over the front-line trenches of the Gordon Highlanders. On the following day, 6 other ranks were killed during heavy shelling. They were relieved that night and moved to Locre. During the winter of 1914-1915 the 3rd Division quickly adapted to the requirements of trench warfare. On 19th December 2nd Lieutenant H.D. Hilton was killed in action at

Kemmel, aged 31 (or 32). However, the war diary states that he was killed at Kemmel on 21st December 1914 He had been master at University College School, Hampstead and had joined the Middlesex Regiment from the University College contingent in September 1914, having received his commission on 6th August 1914. Buried: Kemmel Chateau Military Cemetery, Heuvelland, Belgium.

HOOKHAM, Ernest Edward

Born at Chorleywood on 25th January 1880 and baptized there on 24th March 1800, son of Rosetta, enlisted at Bedford, lived at 'Springwell, Harefield'. G/50145, Private, 11th Middlesex Regiment. Formerly G/41422, Royal Fusiliers. Died of wounds on 12th March 1917, aged 37. He may have been wounded on 26th February when, during preparations for the offensives at Arras were taking place, six platoons of the 11th Middlesex Regiment raided the German trenches. Up until and after 1st March when there were some casualties in the trenches, there were no other reports of other casualties. Husband of Beatrice F. Hookham, nee Collins, of 2, Springwell Cottages, Rickmansworth, Herts, whom he had married in 1905. He is commemorated on the Church Memorial at Harefield. George H. Hookham who was also born at Chorleywood and also lived at Rickmansworth, serving with the 1st Bedfordshire Regiment who was killed in action west of Ypres on 21st April 1915 was probably his cousin. George is commemorated on the war memorial at St. Mary's Church at Rickmansworth, but Ernest is not. Ernest is buried in Habarcq Communal Cemetery Extension Pas de Calais, France.

HUMPHREYS, Edwin Lawrence

Born Kensington, enlisted at Marylebone in September 1914, of Harefield. 11853, Lance-Corporal, 'D' Coy., 2nd Wiltshire Regiment. On 7th October 1914, they had landed at Zeebrugge and had taken part in a few small skirmishes when on 10th March 1915 the 2nd Wilts were in their assembly position at Cameron Lane and had taken part in the magnificent, although minor, victory at Neuve Chapelle. It was their first big attack of the War. Two days later early in the morning, a bombing attack effected a lodgement in the Wiltshire trenches and in a German counter-attack and an advance, after a German trench had just been captured, they were returned out of the firing line across open space between the trenches near St. Eloi which was subjected to artillery attacks in which several men were killed After heavy fighting and several counter-attacks, one company of the Wilts were relieved, the rest of the Battalion had to stay in the line for another 24 hours, suffering many more casualties. During the night of 11th-12th March, the Germans had brought up large reinforcements, including the whole of the 6th Bavarian Reserve Division (which included the 16th Bavarian Infantry Reserve Regiment- the regiment in which Adolf had been serving since the end of October 1914) and several battalions of XIXth (Saxon) Army Corps from Tourcoing, besides concentrating a considerable force of artillery to support the counter-attack. British troops were now reduced to the defensive. He was killed by a shell on 12th March 1915 and reported as missing. An extremely heavy bombardment had heralded that morn. Youngest son of Mr. and Mrs. Humphreys of Trafalgar Place, Kensington, before joining up he had been chauffeur to Mr. Janson of the Dower House, Harefield. He had also worked on the Breakspeare Estate and is commemorated on the Breakspear Estate Memorial. He is also commemorated on St. Mary's War Memorial. Commemorated: Le Touret Memorial, Pas de Calais, France.

IVE, Albert
Born Harefield, enlisted at Uxbridge on 31st August 1914, of Moor Hall, Harefield. 2431, Private, 9th Royal Fusiliers. On the afternoon of Sunday 3rd October 1915, the fighting at Loos which had died down, broke out once more. The front line on this date was formed by the 9th French Corps, occupying Loos, the 12th Division up to the Vermelles-Hulluch road, and the 28th Division. Albert was killed instantly by shrapnel in action in the Hulluch Road trenches near Vermelles at the Battle of Loos on the night of 17th (or 19th) October 1915, during some very heavy shelling, aged 24. During the night of 13th/14th October 1915, the 9th Royal Fusiliers had taken over part of the captured trenches of the Quarries. For the following few days small bombing actions took place as they were consolidating the lines and making communication trenches through the then newly captured area at Loos. On 17th October hostile artillery was very active as it was up until they were relived on 21st. He had worked at the Denham Fishery Estate and had played football for the Moor

Hall Football Club. He does not appear to be commemorated on any of the local memorials. Commemorated: Loos Memorial, Pas de Calais, France.

IVE, B.

He is commemorated on the War Memorial and also on the Church Memorial. **(IVES, B.** on Harefield War Memorial). Brother of Harry Ive(s) – Bertie or William. POSSIBLY Royal Navy.

IVE, Edward

Born Harefield on 14th December 1885, son of George and Emily Ives of Moor Hall. He was educated at Harefield School which he entered on 25th June 1894, enlisted at Hounslow. 25599, Gunner, Royal Garrison Artillery (Royal Regiment of Artillery (RGA) Corps.). Died in the Persian Gulf on 1st May 1916, aged 30. Brother of George Ive and cousin of William Tucker. He is not commemorated locally. Buried: Amara War Cemetery, Iraq.

IVE, George Robert

Born at Harefield on 7th July 1880 and baptized there on 22nd August 1880, lived at Windsor. S/196, Private, 2nd Royal Fusiliers. Killed in action at the Battle of Gully Ravine as the men of X, Y and Z companies advanced beyond the high ground above the sea, known ever after as Fusilier Bluff on 28th June 1915, aged 34. Most of the casualties were caused by shrapnel fire and a few from bullet wounds. Son of George and Emily Ive of Windsor, formerly of Harefield; brother of Edward, above, and cousin of William Tucker. George had served in the South African War, serving as 5288 in the

Gloucestershire Regiment, having joined in March 1900. After the war ended he served in India. He had previously been a labourer. In about 1912 he was discharged on reserve. He does not appear to be commemorated locally, although he is listed in the SSFA document as living at Harefield when he enlisted. Commemorated: Helles Memorial.

IVE, Henry Edward (Harry)
Born Harefield on 27th June 1884, and baptized at Harefield on 27th July 1884, enlisted at Harefield on 5th September 1916, lived at Harefield. T4/216262, Private, Royal Army Service Corps, attd. 202nd Siege Bty. Ammunition Col, Royal Garrison Artillery. Died of wounds on 22nd April 1918, aged 34. He was attached to the Motor Transport of the AMC, and received a fatal wound in the abdomen and left thigh from a shell. He was brought 20th Casualty Clearing Station at Vignacourt on 21st and died the following day. Eldest son of Harry and Emily Martha Ive of Halfway House, Harefield. He was their second son to be killed. He was educated at Harefield School which he joined from the infants on 16th June 1891. He left in March 1895 and before enlistment he had worked for the British Portland Cement Co. at Harefield as a labourer. He is commemorated on Harefield War Memorial as H. Ives and on St. Mary's Church Memorial at Ive, H. Buried: Vignacourt British Cemetery, Somme, D.10, France.

JELLIS, Arnold Walter
Born at Aldbury in Hertfordshire in about 1897, enlisted at Watford, of Harefield. 83032, A/Acting Bombardier. 'C' Bty., 72nd Brigade, Royal Field Artillery. He had gone to France on 27th July 1915

and was killed in action during the Third Battle of Ypres somewhere between the sea and just south of Nieuport, north of the Ypres-Comines Canal on 30th August 1917, aged 21. Son of Walter and Alice Jellis of 17 Barrack Road, Aldbury, Tring. He may have been buried close to where he fell and later reburied in the larger graveyard. He is not commemorated locally. Buried: Coxyde Military Cemetery, Koksijde, West Vlaanderen, Belgium.

JOYCE, Henry William
Born on 5th January 1887, son of Samuel, and was educated at Harefield School from 25th June 1894. 319293, Private, 743rd Area Employment Coy. Labour Corps. Died of pneumonia on 17th February 1919, aged 30. Son of Samuel and Mary Joyce of Watts Common, Harefield; husband of Ethel Beatrice Lily (nee Cripps) Joyce, whom he had married at Hillingdon on July 31st 1915, of 2 Pole Hill Road Cottages, Hillingdon Heath. He is commemorated on St. John's Church, Memorial at Hillingdon and on Harefield War Memorial and St. Mary's Church Memorial at Harefield. His nephew, Frederick Ernest Joyce who lived at Harefield and who was serving with the 3rd London Yeomanry, was killed in action or died of wounds in Italy during World War Two on 2nd October 1943. Henry is buried at Uxbridge (Hillingdon) Cemetery. The inscription on his headstone reads: 'Lo, I am always with you'.

KELLAWAY, F.E.
He is commemorated on the Bell's United Asbestos War Memorial.

KEMPSTER, Albert

Born at Harefield on 4th February 1891, where he was baptized on 29th March 1891, son of Joseph, lived at

Moor Hall, enlisted at Uxbridge on 31st August 1914. 2438, Private, 9th Royal Fusiliers. In the early part of 1915 he was sent to France where he died of wounds received at Loos on 18th October 1915, aged 24. On 14th October 1915, the 9th Royal Fusiliers had moved up to the German old line from trenches near Hulloch. They had taken almost 5 hours to cover roughly one mile. For the following three days they took part in small local bombing actions, without result. From 16th October 1915 there had been heavy shelling for several days in retaliation. Brother of James, below. Husband of Helen Amy Kempster of 61 Barretts Green Road, Acton Lane, Harlesden. He had been educated at Harefield schools, joining the infants' on 1st June 1899. He had married Helen Amy Hull at St. Michael's Church, Stonebridge, on 16th May 1915. He is commemorated on Harefield War Memorial and on St. Mary's Church Memorial at Harefield. The map shown does not include the 12th Division, which included the 9th Royal Fusiliers, but does show the area around Loos. Buried: Vermelles British Cemetery, Pas de Calais, France.

KEMPSTER, Frederick

Born at Harefield on 21st or 22nd November 1888 and baptized at Harefield on 30th December 1888, son of Daniel and Mary Ann Kempster. 144808, Sapper, Royal Engineers. Died from malignant endicarditis at St. Bartholomew's Hospital on 22nd January 1921, aged 32. He had been discharged from the Army and was working as a general labourer. Husband of Mary Ann Kempster of 17 Park Terrace, Harefield. Brother of George and stepbrother of Harry Branch. Fred had been educated at Harefield Schools, joining from the infants' on 1st June 1896. He is commemorated on St. Mary's Church Memorial at Harefield. Buried: Harefield (St. Mary) Churchyard.

KEMPSTER, George Daniel

Born on 17th November 1885 and baptized at Harefield on about 28th February 1886, son of Daniel and Mary Ann. He was educated at Harefield School which he joined from the infants' on 29th July 1893. Formerly G/75216, a Private in the Middlesex Regiment, he had left the Army and died at Springfield Mental Hospital from general paralysis of the insane on 27th December 1919, aged 33. He lived at Rose and Crown Yard, High Street, Harefield, had been under treatment at Tooting Hospital for a time. He is commemorated on St. Mary's Church Memorial. Buried: Harefield (St. Mary) Churchyard.

KEMPSTER, James

Born at Harefield on 1st August 1894, enlisted Harefield. 28007, Private, 11th Suffolk Regiment. Died in France on 6th April 1917, aged 23. He may have been wounded in the Arras right sector of the front line between 24th and 28th March when 4 'other ranks' were killed and 3 wounded, or between 28th March and 31st March at Louez where one 'other  rank' was wounded in a working party when carrying ammunition. Son of Joseph and Sophia Kempster of 7 King's Cottages, Moor Hall, Harefield. Educated at schools in Harefield. He is commemorated on Harefield War Memorial and also commemorated on the Bell's United Asbestos War Memorial. Buried: Aubigny Communal Cemetery Extension, Pas de Calais, K.39, France.

KING, Edwin Edward Robert
Born at Harefield on 7th January 1899 and lived at Harefield, enlisted at Uxbridge on 26th November 1913, giving his age as just over 17. T.F.2300, Private, 1/8th Middlesex Regiment. Killed in action during the Battle of the Somme at Souastre near Leuze Wood on or after 17th July 1916, aged 16. On that day attempted raids had been made, but the enemy was found to be too alert. Son of Edwin Robert and Mary Ann King of 1 Waterloo Villas, High Street, Harefield. Educated at schools in Hillingdon and Harefield, after which he became a greengrocer. He is commemorated on Harefield War Memorial and on St. Mary's Church Memorial. Commemorated: Thiepval Memorial, Somme, France.

KINTISH, J.
He is commemorated on the Bell's United Asbestos War Memorial.

KNIGHT, W.

He is commemorated on the Bell's United Asbestos War Memorial.

LAMB, George William

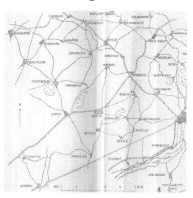 Born West Hyde, Herts., on 20th May 1887 and baptized at Harefield on 31st May 1887, son of Eldred and (Mary) Jane Lamb, enlisted Uxbridge, lived at Harefield. Private, G/57120, 9th Royal Fusiliers. He was a stretcher-bearer. On 23rd April 1918, the 12th Division moved forward, relieving the New Zealand Division on that portion of the line covering Mailly Maillet and Auchonvillers. On the night of May 24th 1918, the eve of the assault at Loos, he had just helped carry in several badly wounded men under intense fire, when he was hit. His body was recovered 2 days later and buried at Mailly-Maillet. He was 31 years old, the son of Mr. Eldred Lamb and Mrs. Lamb of Breakspear Road, Harefield and husband of Lily Elizabeth Lamb, nee Sims, of 86, Maple Road, Luton. They had married in 1914. He was educated at Harefield School which he joined from the infants on 5th June 1895. At some time he had been a gardener, probably on the Breakspear Estate. Brother of Percy Lamb. He is commemorated on the Bell's United Asbestos War Memorial as well as on Harefield War Memorial, on St. Mary's Memorial and the Breakspear Estate

Memorial. The map shows the area around Mailly-Maillet. Buried: Mailly Wood Cemetery, Maillet Maillet, Somme, France.

LAMB, Percy, MM

Born Harefield, enlisted at Uxbridge on 9th September 1914, lived at Harefield. 6117, Sergeant, 8th Royal Fusiliers. Killed in action near Monchy-le-Preux on 1st September 1917. He was out wiring with 6 or so others at the time when a shell from artillery fire fell close to them – 'caught by a salvo of whizz bangs' as they were returning to their section. Three were killed and 3 wounded. He had already been wounded 6 times, the first time on his 21st birthday. Three times he was treated in English hospitals, and three times he received field hospital treatment. Awarded the Military Medal in early 1917 for taking a German trench and holding it for 39 hours, in the interim causing the enemy heavy casualties. He had been employed at the Asbestos Works, as had his father, and is commemorated their War Memorial. He is also commemorated on Harefield War Memorial and on the Church memorial and on the Breakspeare Estate Memorial. Son of Eldred, who died on 13th April 1928, and Mary Lamb and younger brother of George. Buried: Monchy British Cemetery, Monchy-le-Preux, Pas de Calais, France.

LAMBART, Gerald Edgar Oliver Fortescue

Born at Dublin on 30th November 1885, elder son of Colonel Edgar Lambart of Fouracres, Harefield. Major, 1st Royal Scots Fusiliers. Died in hospital

41

near Poperinghe on 28th March 1916, from wounds received in the trenches in action near St. Eloi the  previous day, aged 30. A small salient had been formed east of St. Eloi, known as the Mound, important for artillery observation. It was known to be strongly held and the task for attacking it was given to the 3rd Division. At 4.15am on 27th March five mines in front of St. Eloi were sprung and almost immediately enemy artillery opened, bombarding the front line trenches for two hours before slacking off at about 6.30. He had been educated at Laleham, Eton and the Royal Military College, Sandhurst, gazetted 2nd Lieutenant in the 19th Hussars on 28th January 1905, promoted Lieutenant on 20th February 1907 and attached to the North Nigerian Regiment, WAFF in 1910, and Captain, 2nd September 1912. He served with the Expeditionary Force from May 1915, in West Africa and France and volunteered for the infantry in August and transferred to the Royal Scots Fusiliers when he was promoted temporary Major in March 1916. He is commemorated on both the Harefield War Memorial and St. Mary's Church Memorial. Buried: Lijssenthoek Military Cemetery, Belgium.

LAMBOURNE, J.

He is commemorated on the Bell's United Asbestos War Memorial and is also commemorated on St. Mary's Church memorial at Rickmansworth as J.M. Lambourne. He was serving as a Private with the 36th Field Ambulance, Royal Army Medical Corps and was killed in action on 21st August 1916 and buried in Faubourg d'Amiens Cemetery at Arras..

LANE, C.
He is commemorated on Harefield War Memorial and on the Church Memorial. Possibly William Lane, below.

LANE, William Charles
Born at Denham, enlisted Mill Hill, of Harefield. G/21984, Private, 17th Middlesex Regiment. Killed in action in the front line near Bourlon in a bombardment of gradually increasing intensity, at the Battle of Cambrai on 2nd December 1917 in attacks on Ernst and Edda Weg communication trenches. Between 30th November 1917 when the 17th Middlesex were in a furious fight near the Canal du Nord and 2nd/3rd December, the 17th Middlesex casualties had been heavy. At 3.30 in the afternoon of 2nd December the enemy commenced shelling on our front and support lines and at 4.30 heavy rifle fire was heard. One hour later the shelling, which had been very accurate, ceased and the night was fairly quiet. Commemorated: Cambrai Memorial, Louveral, Nord, France.

LAURIER, W.D.
He is commemorated on the Bell's United Asbestos War Memorial.

LENNOX, M.
He is commemorated on the Bell's United Asbestos War Memorial.

LITTLE, J.
He is commemorated on Harefield War Memorial and on the Church Memorial. He had enlisted after the beginning of 1916.

LOFTY, Herbert Henry

Born at Harefield on 24th June 1896, enlisted at  Harefield on January 24th 1916. G/11882, Sergeant, 19th Middlesex Regiment. He had been promoted Corporal on 24th September 1916, appointed Lance Sergeant on 27th October 1916 and promoted to Sergeant on 3rd November 1916. He was killed in action at Messines on the second day of the battle, on 8th June 1917, aged 21. The capture of Messines Ridge in June 1917 was one of the most successful British operations on the Western Front and had tactical value for the British Army in that area – the Ypres salient was a death trap. Messines Ridge could be captured in the course of one attack, and casualties were comparatively light as the Germans had been surprised when the mines under their trenches were blown. He had been wounded slightly in the hand and back on 7th June and told to stop and rest. However he insisted on going out with his platoon the next day when he was caught by a small piece of shell in the neck in one of the counter-attacks and died instantly. Son of Henry and Florence Lofty of 1 New Cottages, Park Lane, Harefield. He was educated at Harefield schools and was formerly employed as an asbestos cutter at the Asbestos Works where he is commemorated. He is also commemorated on both war memorials at Harefield – the village memorial and the Church memorial. Buried: Dickebusch New Military Cemetery Extension, C.18, Belgium.

LOFTY, James Henry

Born Harefield, enlisted Mill Hill. P.W. 5263, Private, 26th Middlesex Regiment. The Regiment went to Salonika in August 1916 where he died, probably in the 40th Casualty Clearing Station on 8th December 1916. He may have been wounded at the Battle of Tumbitza Farm between 6th and 7th December 1916 or may have died of disease. Possibly James Lofty, son of George of Hill End, born on 2nd January 1886 and educated at Harefield Schools, which he joined from the infants' on 26th June 1893. He is commemorated on both the War Memorial and St. Mary's Church Memorial. Buried: Struma Military Cemetery V.J.4

LOFTY, Sydney John

Born on 10th July 1898, son of Henry and Florence  Susan Lofty of 1 New Cottages, Park Lane, Harefield. 304975, Sapper, "F" Coy. 1st Reserve Battalion Royal Engineers. He was taken ill in about January 1918 and died of tubercular pleurisy of the right lung, and consolidation of the right lung, probably tubercular portal congestion due to the enlargement of the liver and spleen, at the VAD Hospital at Northwood on 9th January 1919, aged 19. He had been educated at Harefield schools. He is commemorated on Harefield War Memorial and on St. Mary's Church Memorial. Buried: St. Mary's Church, Harefield.

LOFTY, William Richard

Born at Harefield on 26th April 1892, lived at

Harefield, enlisted Marylebone. 13384, Private, 2nd Bedfordshire Regiment. Killed in action near Roupy during the German spring offensive at St. Quentin on 22nd March 1918. The German Crown Prince had ordered that Tertry road should be reached by his troops, which involved the seizure of the Holnon plateau. On 21st March, the first day of the attack, the 2nd Bedfords held their entire battle zone for the whole day, having given up their front line positions early on and concentrating on the second line of defense. On the following day this defense collapsed at the left and right of the division and was pushed back. The 2nd Bedfords, who were holding the front of the Battle Zone, suffered severe losses in a very heavy attack, including Private Lofty. Son of Mr. W. Lofty of 1 King's Cottages, Moor Hall, Harefield. Educated at Harefield schools. He is commemorated on Harefield War Memorial and on the Church Memorial. There is also a W.R. Lofty who is commemorated on the memorial at St. Mary's Church, Rickmansworth. Buried: Chapelle British Cemetery, Aisne, A.6. France.

LOOM, O.

He is commemorated on the Bell's United Asbestos War Memorial.

LUCAS, Joseph

Born at Yiewsley on 3rd March 1887, son of James Frederick and Ellen Lucas, enlisted Hounslow, of Harefield. L/987, Private, 8th Royal Fusiliers. Pending the general attack at Loos, local operations were carried out to recover the Dump and Fosse 8 near Auchy. During the first week of October 1915, a  large amount of work carried out by the 12th Division was entailed in consolidating the lines and in making communication trenches of 2,000 to 3,000 yards through the newly captured area near Loos. On the afternoon of 3rd October 1915, fighting, which had died down, broke out once more. On this date, the front line was formed by the 9th French Corps on the right, occupying Loos and that portion of the slopes of Hill 70 which still remained in our hands. On their left was the 12th Division up to the Vermelles-Hulluch road. On 4th October he was killed in action by artillery fire in the trenches at Vermelles. On that date, the 8th Royal Fusiliers secured a better site on the Lens-la-Bassee road by bombing. Trench warfare methods had been undertaken with heavy casualties on both sides. He was educated at Harefield School which he joined from the infants' on 1st June 1896, and had served with the Expeditionary Force. He is commemorated on the Bell's United Asbestos War Memorial and on the Harefield War Memorial and the Church Memorial. The illustration shows the area around La Bassee. Son of James Lucas of Hill End, Harefield. Commemorated: Loos Memorial, Pas de Calais, France.

MARSDEN, G.
Of Harefield, where he is commemorated on the War Memorial and on the Church memorial.

A George Marsden lived at The Shrubs, Harefield. Possibly George MARSTON, born at Watford, enlisted at Northwood, of Northwood. 83107, Private, 139th Coy., Northamptonshire Regiment, Labour Corps. Formerly 32864, Middlesex Regiment. Killed in action on 28th February 1918. Buried: Duhallows Advanced Dressing Station Cemetery, Ieper, Belgium.

MARSDEN, T.
He is commemorated on Harefield War Memorial. Probably a mistake for Thomas MARSTON below.

MARSHALL, George
Born Trowbridge, enlisted Hounslow, of Harefield. L/8542, Private, 4th Royal Fusiliers. The Battalion had been in action on the Aisne and after they were relieved by French troops on 2nd October 1914, they hurried 80 miles north to Ypres where they were in action around Aubers Ridge and Neuve Chapelle. In the winter of 1914/15 they experienced the hardships of trench life. On Wednesday June 16th 1915, they were in action to the immediate north of Hooge. The 9th Brigade were in reserve near Poperinghe but was brought forward through Ypres for the assault. A pause of nearly 3 weeks followed during which time there was sporadic fighting. On 19th June the Battalion moved to trenches in Sanctuary Wood at Ypres and on 20th June 1915, the Germans shelled Sanctuary Wood heavily from time to time throughout the day. The next four days were quite quiet, but he was reported to have been killed in action here in Flanders on 24th June 1915. He had worked on the Breakspeare Estate and is commemorated on their memorial. He is also

commemorated on Harefield War Memorial and Harefield Church of St Mary's memorial. Commemorated: Ypres (Menin Gate) Memorial, Ieper, West Vlaanderen, Belgium.

MARSHALL, Walter Forsyth
Born Trowbridge, Wilts., enlisted Fulham. 86144, Gunner, 5th Brigade, Royal Field Artillery. Wounded in action by gunshot in his right side on about 18th September 1918 near Briseux Wood and died on 24th October 1918 at the 1st Southern General Hospital, Edgbaston, from empyaema, aged 26. Son of Aaron and Elizabeth Marshall of Vine Cottage, Breakspear Road, Harefield and brother of George, above. He had worked on the Breakspeare Estate as an agricultural labourer. He is commemorated on the Breakspear Estate Memorial and also on Harefield War Memorial and on the Church Memorial. Buried: Birmingham (Lodge Hill) Cemetery, Warwickshire.

MARSTON, George
Brother of Thomas. See George MARSDEN

MARSTON, Thomas
Born Harefield, enlisted Warminster, Wilts., resided  at Uxbridge. 25857, Private, 5th Wiltshire Regiment. In February 1916, the 5th Wilts went by sea to Basra via Kuwait. In March they continued up the River Tigris in barges to Amara. From here they went up-river to relieve the Lahore Division south of Kut, where they attempted to break through the Turkish Division which was besieging Kut. By the middle of February they were established on the southern bank

of the Tigris near Kut. On 23rd, the river was crossed west of the town and by the end of the month were nearing Baghdad. On 29th March, the Battalion advanced on the enemy near Daltawa, north of Baghdad. The Wiltshires moved under shell fire to a deep nullah, almost one mile ahead. From here on, the ground was completely open and enfiladed by machine-gun fire from the Turkish position a mile away. Casualties were heavy. It was here that he was probably wounded and died of wounds in Mara, Mesopotamia on 29th March 1917. After his death, the family was evicted from their tied cottage in Warminster where he had worked as a gardener. Commemorated: Basra Memorial, Iraq.

MESSENGER, J.
He is commemorated on the Bell's United Asbestos War Memorial.

MILES, Alfred
Born Harefield, enlisted Mill Hill. 96740, Private, 10th Tank Corps. He was killed in action on March 25th 1918, aged 18. On 20th March 1918 prisoners from various different German regiments had been captured near St. Quentin and left the British in no doubt about an attack beginning the following day. He may have been killed in one of the seven tanks of the 10th Tank Corps which came from Logeast Wood on that day on the northern flank of the Germans near Grevillers. Only two of the seven tanks came out of the action. Formerly 1532, 21st Battalion Training Reserve. He was the youngest son of Mr. and Mrs. Robert Miles and brother of John Robert Miles, of Filicol Lodge, 26 Mount Pleasant, Harefield. He is commemorated on Harefield War Memorial and on

the Church Memorial. Commemorated: Arras Memorial, Pas de Calais, France.

MILES, D.

He is commemorated on Harefield War Memorial and on the Church Memorial. There are no D. Miles recorded in the SSFA document, which lists all men from Harefield who joined the Army or Navy prior to the end of 1915 or the beginning of 1916.

MILES, John Robert

 Born on 4th September 1889 and educated at Harefield School, joining the infants' school on 1st June 1897. He had served in the Navy for over 5 years and had been discharged when his time was up. He lived at the Gelantine Works, Harefield and enlisted at Ealing on 22nd July 1915. T.F.241394, Private, 1/8th Middlesex Regiment. He was appointed (acting) Lance Corporal on 7th August 1915 but deprived of his Lance stripe on 24th September 1915. He had been wounded in action twice in 1916 and had suffered from shell-shock. On August 16th 1917 Zero Hour was at 4.45am, the object being the carrying of Nonnebosch and Glencorse. The 1/8th Middlesex advanced in three waves amidst hostile machine-gun and rifle fire across the valley near the Westhoek Ridge. German aeroplanes machine-gunned troops who were sheltering in an exposed position and at 1pm for two hours, enemy guns opened fire on the Middlesex heavily and there were many casualties. Private Miles was killed in action at the battle of Lens during the Third Battle of Ypres on this day, 'whilst attempting to save the life of a comrade'; or ('while

rendering very fine valuable service as a runner'). So serious were the losses of the 56th Division that the 14th Division took its place on the following day. He was aged 29, the second son of Mr. Robert and Mrs. Sarah Miles of Filicol Lodge, Harefield. He does not appear to be commemorated on Harefield Memorials but is mentioned in the SSFA documents as being of Harefield. Commemorated: Tyne Cot Memorial, Zonnebeke, West Vlaanderen, Belgium.

MONTAGUE, John Butler
Born at Harefield on 29th February 1884 and baptized

there on 25th May 1884, son of William and Sophia, lived at Harefield where he enlisted on 7th June 1916. 5281, Private, 9th Royal Fusiliers.

Monchy

On 17th June 1917, the 12th Division commenced moving back to Arras and on the night of 19th-20th took over the front line, running in a semicircle about 1,000 yards east of Monchy le Preux from the 3rd Division. Enemy aeroplanes were very active and Hook Trench and Monchy were frequently shelled by, amongst others, the 26th Infantry Division (Wurtembergers). On the morning of 30th June 1917 at Monchy, he was instantly killed by a trench-mortar shell fired by the enemy from Bois du Vert. Son of William; husband of J. (Catherine) Montague of Chapel Row, Harefield. He was educated at Harefield School, which he had joined from the infants' on 22nd June 1891 and had previously worked at the Asbestos Works where he is commemorated. He is also commemorated on Harefield War Memorial and Harefield Church Memorial. Buried: Monchy British Cemetery, Pas de Calais, France, F.9.

NEWMAN, J. (or T.)
He is commemorated on the Bell's United Asbestos War Memorial. J. Newman is also commemorated on the memorial at St. Mary's Church, Rickmansworth.

NINNIS, Thomas
Born at Treers, Cornwall, enlisted at Harefield. 198523, Bombardier Ninnis died of wounds in hospital in France on 30th August 1918, aged 29. He was for many years employed by Mr. Beckley (a baker) and had lived in Harefield for many years. He was first of all in the Royal Army Veterinary Corps (SE/17312), but was later transferred to the Royal Field Artillery, and later to the trench mortars. Y/74th Medium Trench Mortar Bty., Royal Field Artillery. He is commemorated on Harefield War Memorial. Buried: Les Baraques Military Cemetery, Sangatte,

OWEN, Frederick W.
Born Clapton, Northants., enlisted Hounslow. 54901, Private, 4th Grenadier Guards. The 4th Grenadier Guards were in action in Bourlon Wood and south-east of it on 24th November 1917. At nightfall on the following day they were relieved and moved back to the south-east corner of Bourlon Wood. By the 29th November they were in Trescault near where they pitched tents which they occupied for the night and on the following day repitched their tents in

Havrincourt Wood. He was killed in action near Masnieres at the Battle of Cambrai on 1st December 1917, aged 30, when the tactical plans of the German command were thwarted. In a resumed attack on the morning of that date, the Guards recaptured Gonnelieu and together with dismounted cavalry cleared Gauche Wood in heavy shelling. The attack started at 6.30am. The Germans began accurately machine-gunning the men as they advanced over open ground and up a gentle incline leading to Gonnelieu. The fire was terrific. Son of William Owen of Thrapston, Northants; husband of Minnie Louisa Owen of 25 Park Terrace, Harefield. He is commemorated on Harefield War Memorial. Commemorated: Cambrai Memorial, Louveral, Nord, France.

OWEN, W.

He is commemorated on the Church Memorial. As there is no such name on the SSFA document, which records all men from Harefield who had enlisted in the Army or Navy prior to early 1916, he must have joined up after that, or be a mistake for Frederick Owen, above

PACKHAM, George

Born Merstham, Surrey, enlisted at Marylebone soon after the outbreak of war, of Merstham. 11852, Lance/Corporal, 5th Wiltshire Regiment. He served in France and Salonica. In March 1916 he went with the 13th Division to join the Relief of Kut expedition. In the attempt to relieve Kut on 5th April 1916, the 5th Wilts went over the top at dawn and drove the enemy out of three lines of trenches, advancing to Falahiyeh where he was killed in action on that date, aged 28. Just before dawn the bombardment began and at 4.55am the newly arrived 13th Division attacked the Hanna positions and captured the Turkish first and second lines and, after the guns had lifted, swept forward into the Turkish third lines, which were found the be empty. The Hanna positions had been captured with little opposition. He had been a member of the Harefield Cricket Club and was a splendid bowler. Son of Mr. and Mrs. P.R. Packham of Railway Cottages, Merstham, Surrey. He is commemorated on Harefield War Memorial and on Harefield Church Memorial. Commemorated: Basra Memorial, Iraq.

PADDON, F.
He is commemorated on the Bell's United Asbestos War Memorial.

PAINTER, Alfred

Born and lived at Harefield, enlisted Whitehall. G/14875, Private, 10th The Buffs (East Kent Regiment). Died of wounds, probably in one of the CCS in or near Lapugnoy, on 18th October 1918, aged 19. He may have been wounded in the Lys valley in one of the last fights in France. On 4th October they were held up along the railway from Lille to La Bassee where fighting took place. They were again in action on 16th October near Lille, where they advanced at 6.30, pressing on north-east to Ascq where they encountered strong resistance from behind a railway embankment west of the River Marcq. Son of Alfred and Mary Painter of Lodge Farm Cottage, Harefield.

He is commemorated on Harefield War Memorial and on the Church Memorial. Buried: Lapugnoy Military Cemetery, Pas de Calais, C.7, France.

PEVERILL, John
Born at Harefield on 24th November 1894, son of Henry Peverill of 28, Moorhall Road, enlisted at Mill Hill and lived at Harefield where he was educated. G/23147, Private, 6th Middlesex Regiment, part of the Thames and Medway Garrison. He had been injured in January 1917 and taken to the Temporary Military Hospital at Edmonton where he died from sarcoma of the tonsil on 4th April 1917, aged 22. He is commemorated on both the Church and the War Memorials at Harefield. Buried: Harefield (St. Mary) Churchyard.

PRITCHARD, Edward
Born Bushey, enlisted in London, of New Years  Green Road. Private, 7776, 1st Royal Scots Fusiliers. The 1st Scots Fusiliers had been in action at Mons on 23rd August 1914 against the enemy 6th and 17th Divisions and the 18 Jaeger Division. As the Germans advanced through Belgium, the British Army retreated from Mons and between 28th and 30th August the 3rd Division marched 68 miles in 50 hours. By 14th September they were crossing the Aisne. Between 15th September at Vailly and 23rd September 1914 there were a series of counter-attacks. At some time he was captured and died of wounds on 15th September 1914, whilst a Prisoner of War in the hands of the Germans. He had served with the Expeditionary Force. Son of Edward and Mary

Pritchard. He is recorded in the SSFA document as of Harefield at the time of his enlistment, although he does not appear on any war memorial. Commemorated: La Ferte-sous-Jouarre Memorial, Seine-et Marne, France.

PURSER, Sidney Charles
Born Harefield, enlisted in the Middlesex Regiment at Harefield in January 1916, of Harefield. He later transferred to 'D' Coy., X111 Platoon, 2nd Royal Sussex Regiment as G/17739, Private. He had been hit by a bullet while out on patrol on 10th March 1917 and reported as missing on that day and on the following day was reported as killed in action, although the Red Cross and Order of St. John Enquiry List of the Wounded and Missing record him as missing on 14th March 1917. Indeed, the war diary of the 2nd Sussex Regiment records that on 10th March 1917 they had moved back into support prior to a bombardment. A Fighting Patrol was sent out to try to secure a prisoner on this day, whilst Barleux Quarry was intensely bombarded. This patrol was unsuccessful. Two men were wounded and one missing. He served with the British Expeditionary Force. Formerly Middlesex Regiment, which he joined in January 1916 later transferring to the 2nd Royal Fusiliers. Son of Mr. William Purser of The Old School House, Harefield, later of High Street, Harefield. He was educated at Harefield schools and prior to enlisting he had been a groom at Breakspeares. He had gone to France in July 1916. He is commemorated on the Breakspear Estate Memorial and on both St. Mary's Memorial and the village memorial. Commemorated: Thiepval Memorial, Somme, France.

QUIRK, H.

He is commemorated on the Bell's United Asbestos War Memorial.

RANCE, Henry Richard

 Born Chertsey, enlisted Harefield, lived at 2 Park Terrace, Harefield. 474712, Sapper, 4 S 518th Field Coy., Royal Engineers. Killed in action between 21st and 22nd March 1918, aged 28. He was one of a party sent out to occupy a trench on the Somme. Only one of the party returned. He had been in France for nearly one year and had at first been reported as missing. Son of Jonathan and Lucy Rance of 'The Vernon Arms' Hill End, Harefield; husband of Eliza Rance of 2 Park Terrace, Harefield. He is commemorated on Harefield War Memorial and on the Church Memorial. Buried: Fins New British Cemetery, Somme, E.23, France.

RANCH, H.

He is commemorated on the Bell's United Asbestos War Memorial. Maybe a mistake for Harry Branch. More than likely a mistake for Henry Rance.

REEVES, Frederick William

Born Harlesden on 19th June 1899 and baptized there at All Soul's on 18th August 1899, son of Rosa, enlisted in London, of Hill End, Harefield. G/68773, Private, Royal West Surrey Regiment, 1/22nd London Battalion, although the CWGC gives his regiment as 1/22nd Queen's Royal West Surrey Regiment (which doesn't seem to exist). Died of severe wounds in No. 22 or No. 20 Casualty Clearing Station on 1st

September 1918, aged 19. No. 20 CCS seems the most likely as it was situated at Heilly. Towards the end of August 1918, the Regiment was on the Somme near Montaubon where gas shells were poured on them. He was educated at Harefield Schools and had been a gardener in the employ of Mr. Billyard Leake of Harefield Park. Son of Mrs. R. Baggs (formerly Reeves). He is commemorated on both the village memorial and on the Church memorial. Buried: Heilly Station Cemetery, Mericourt-L'Abbe, Somme, France.

RICHARDSON, Herbert

Born Harefield on 8th August 1894, son of John Precious Richardson and Eliza Richardson, enlisted at Uxbridge soon after war broke out and lived at Uxbridge. 5220, Private, London Regiment 22nd (County of London) Battalion (The Queen's). Formerly 1454, 8th Royal Fusiliers. Killed instantly in action on the Somme near Guedecourt whilst trying to remove the wounded to a place of safety on 6th October 1916. He had served at the Front for some time and was twice wounded. On recovery he was transferred to the Medical Section of the 1/22nd London Regiment. Son of Mrs. Richardson of Belle View Terrace, Harefield and brother younger of Percy, below. Herbert was educated at Harefield schools had worked at the Asbestos Works. He is commemorated on Harefield Wesleyan Church Memorial and on Harefield War Memorial and St. Mary's Church Memorial. Commemorated: Thiepval Memorial, Somme.

RICHARDSON, Percy

Born at Harefield on 5th December 1891, son of John Precious Richardson and his wife Eliza, brother of Herbert, enlisted at Harrow at the end of October 1916, lived at the time of his enlistment at 8 Bell Vue Terrace, Harefield and later, after he had married, at Newbury. 180434, Private, 339 HS Works Coy., Labour Corps. Formerly 71525, Middlesex Regiment. Died of pneumonia following on from influenza contracted on military service at 10.22 on 9th November 1918 in the 2nd Eastern General Hospital at Brighton. He had been educated at Harefield schools after which he became a carpenter. He is commemorated on the Bell's United Asbestos War Memorial. Husband of Flossie, whom he had married at the Wesleyan Chapel at Hampstead on 12th October 1916. Buried: Newbury Old Cemetery, Berkshire.

RICHE, H.A.

He is commemorated on the Bell's United Asbestos War Memorial.

ROGERS, David

 Born on 29th May 1898, son of Mrs. Minnie L. Owen of 25 Park Terrace, Harefield. Officers Steward 3rd Class, L/7600, Royal Naval Air Service (Felixstowe). He had been badly wounded on 4th July 1917 during a daylight air-raid by 18 Gotha aircraft at 0.7.20-25hrs on the east coast, the target of which were both Felixstowe, where considerable damage was done, and Harwich and died of these wounds in Shatley

Hospital on 6th July 1917, aged 19. He had been educated at Harefield School, which he joined from the infants' on 17th June 1907. He is commemorated on both the War Memorial and the Church memorial at Harefield. Buried: Harefield (St. Mary) Churchyard.

RYDER, Frank
Born at Harefield on 11th March 1898, son of James and Emma Ryder of Riverside Cottage, Harefield. He was educated at Harefield schools. He enlisted at Mill Hill in August 1916, serving as Private, 22663, Middlesex Regiment, later transferring to Private, 34583, 8th East Surrey Regiment. Died from wounds received on 8th January 1918, when he was taken prisoner at Houthulst Forest. He was aged 19 and 'buried in the Military Cemetery at Hooglede'. His body was later moved to where he now lies in eternal sleep. Before the war he worked at the Asbestos Works where he is commemorated. He is also commemorated on both the War Memorial and Church memorial at Harefield. Buried: Harlebeke New British Cemetery, Belgium.

SANDS, C.
He is commemorated on the Bell's United Asbestos War Memorial.

SMITH, Alfred William
Born Battersea, enlisted at Uxbridge in 1913, lived at Harefield where he had worked as a labourer at the Asbestos Works. T.F.2120, Private, 'D' Coy., 1/8th Middlesex Regiment. He was a machine gunner. They had come into line on September 9th 1916 after being reformed and reinforced after their awful

ordeal and terrible losses at the Gommecourt Salient on 1st July. On 15th they went forward with the whole line at 6.20 in the morning. It was in this action that he was killed in action at Lesboeufs on 15th September 1916, on the first day of the third and final stage of operations on the Somme at the battle of Flers-Courcelette. The original direction of the advance had been north and south, but it soon became almost from west to east as the Division, pivoting upon Leuze Wood, swung round to attack Bouleaux Wood to the north of it. The 167th Brigade fought its way bravely into the wood, where they endured the usual horrors of this forest fighting. There was very heavy barrage between Ginchy and Bouleaux Wood. He had probably been shot. The advance to Leuze Wood and during an attack at the north-west side of Bouleaux Wood at 1.40pm was greatly helped by the tanks which had been brought into action for the very first time. Casualties, however, were heavy. Eldest son of Mr. Alfred and the late Mrs. Smith of The Lodge, Harefield Grove. He is commemorated on the memorial in St. Mary's Church and on the village green memorial. Commemorated: Thiepval Memorial, Somme, France.

STANTON, J.
He is commemorated on the Bell's United Asbestos War Memorial.

STATHAM, Albert
Born Uxbridge, enlisted Uxbridge, of Harefield. 3480, Private, 13th Royal Fusiliers. Killed in action at Ovillers on 8th July 1916 in the continuing fight for Contalmaison (defended by the 3rd Prussian Guards), Bazentin, Bazentin-le-Grand, Ovillers (held by the

180th Wurtembergers), Trones Wood, Longueval and Delville Wood. At 2am on 7th July the 13th Royal Fusiliers had assembled in the old German line in front of La Boiselle for an attack between Ovillers and Contalmaison where many casualties were caused by German artillery. On the following day

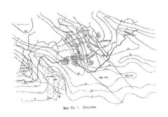

they were ordered to push on to the next line. A small party pushed too far ahead and suffered severely. Possibly Albert Statham, son of William, born on 13th November 1891 who was educated at Harefield School, joining from the infants' school on 1st June 1899. His is commemorated on Harefield's War Memorial and the Church memorial and he is also commemorated on the Bell's United Asbestos War Memorial. Commemorated: Thiepval Memorial, Somme, France.

STATHAM, George Ernest

Born at Harefield on 16th November 1885 and baptized there on 31st January 1886, son of William and Elizabeth. He enlisted at Chinchilla, Queensland. 293, Private, 31st Battalion, Australian Infantry, AIF. Killed in action in the attack on Fromelles, north-east of Aubers, on 20th July 1916, aged 31. The battle of Fromelles on 19-20 July 1916, was a minor, albeit vicious British attack (with two Australian Divisions) which lasted for 16 hours, launched close to Aubers Ridge in order to prevent the Germans moving troops from their quiet sectors to the battle of the Somme. Unfortunately, this attack was delivered on too narrow a front and was advertised by a preliminary bombardment lasting for 5 days. By 5.45am on 20th July 1916, the Australian 8th Brigade had been forced out of the trenches they had captured the evening before. He was educated at Harefield School, which he joined from the infants' on 25th June 1894, and had emigrated to Australia when he was 26 years old and was a railway labourer. Son of the late William (he had died on 4th July 1901, aged 55, and buried at Harefield) and Elizabeth. He is commemorated on Harefield War Memorial and on the Church memorial. Commemorated: VC Corner Australian Cemetery Memorial, Fremelles, Nord, France.

SUDBURY, H.
He is commemorated on the Bell's United Asbestos War Memorial. As he is not commemorated on any village memorial, he lived away from Harefield. Possibly Harry Sudbury, a successful sportsman of Uxbridge who was serving as a Private in the 1/8th Middlesex Regiment and who was killed in action at Zonnebeke on Whit Monday 26th April 1915 in nerve-shattering sniping and bombing which enfiladed them from both flanks, causing many casualties. The condition of the parapets as left by the French meant that no reply was possible on our part. He is commemorated on the Ypres (Menin Gate) Memorial in Belgium.

SWAN, Ernest Albert
Born at Harefield on 7th November 1890 and baptized at Harefield on 25th January 1891, son of Walter and Lucy, lived at Harefield, enlisted Harrow. 26750, Private, 7th Royal Fusiliers (City of London Regiment). Killed in action in France in a major

attack by the Germans near Gavrelle at the Second Battle of the Scarpe on Monday 23rd April 1917, aged 29. The Battalion in the Gavrelle trenches assembled at 9.45am, preparing for the assault. On getting to the enemy lines they found the German wire uncut and were met by German bombing parties, snipers and strong resistance from machine-guns. With twenty tanks in support, extremely fierce fighting was witnessed on this date on a nine-mile front on both banks of the Scarpe against the line Gavrelle-Roeux-Guemappe-Fontaine les Croisilles. On this St. George's Day, there were very heavy losses. The 7th Battalion attacked north of Gavrelle, assisting all the other units of the 63rd (Naval) Division. Son of Walter Swan of 25 Moorhall Cottages, Harefield. He had been educated at Harefield School, transferring from the infants' school on 1st June 1899. He is commemorated on both the War Memorial and the Church memorial. Buried: Orchard Dump Cemetery, Arleux-en-Gohelle, Pas de Calais, B.6, France.

TAYLOR, A.
He is commemorated on Harefield War Memorial and on the Church Memorial. No A. Taylor is listed on the SSFA document as having enlisted in the Army of Navy prior to the beginning of 1916.

TAYLOR, G.
He is commemorated on the Church Memorial. No G. Taylor is listed on the SSFA document as having enlisted into the Army of Navy prior to the beginning of 1916.

TAYLOR, John Robert

Born at Uxbridge on 18th May 1895, son of Walter Taylor. He was educated at Harefield, where he lived and enlisted at Uxbridge on 4th September 1914. 7698, Private, 11th Royal Fusiliers. Formerly 5717, Middlesex Regiment. As July 1st 1916 approached, some complex and successful trench digging had been done on the Somme front. Eight covered saps had been driven forward and reached a point within 20 yards of the German trenches without their knowledge. Upon the advance being ordered, the end of these were opened up, machine-guns and flame-throwers were thrust through and the saps behind were quickly unroofed and turned into communication trenches. On the first day of the Battle of the Somme, 1st July 1916, the Picardy front was to be attacked between the region of Hebuterne and the region of Lassigny (about 70 km) in the general direction of line Bapaume-Peronne-Ham, the British sector had been between about Arras and Albert on the Bapaume Front. The 11th Royal Fusiliers and 7th Bedfordshire led the attack on the southern face of Mametz. They made a rapid advance, stormed the Pommiers Trench and later were in vicious hand-to-hand fighting during the capture of Pommiers Redoubt, Beetle Alley and White Trench. He was killed in action on this day in the capture of Pommiers Redoubt and Montaubon on the opening day of the Battle of the Somme, aged 21. The 18th Division which had done no serious fighting before, established a remarkable record of good service during the whole course of the Somme battle. Stepbrother of Mr. J. East of 10 Moorhall Cottages, Uxbridge. He is commemorated on Harefield War

Memorial. Commemorated: Thiepval Memorial, Somme, France.

THRIFT, Henry John
Born at Harefield on 28th February 1885, son of William and Louisa Thrift, enlisted at Uxbridge on 3rd September 1914, lived at Sidney Cottages, Harefield. G/3274, Sergeant, 12th Middlesex Regiment. He had gone to France in July 1915 and promoted to Lance Corporal on 12th November 1914, Corporal on 11th May 1915 and Sergeant on 9th May 1916. He suffered from shell shock on 30th June 1916. On 29th September 1916 he was appointed Acting Quartermaster Sergeant, which he relinquished on 19th January 1917, on being admitted to hospital. He had been through the battle of the Somme and other battles with his Battalion when he was killed in action at Poelcapelle on 17th-18th October 1917, aged 32, and 'buried in a churchyard on the battlefield', but his body later went missing. He was educated at Harefield School which he had joined from the infants' school on 21st June 1892, afterwards becoming a labourer. He is commemorated on Harefield War Memorial and St. Mary's Church Memorial. Commemorated: Tyne Cot Memorial, Zonnebeke, West Vlaanderen, Belgium.

TUCKER, William James
Born at Harefield on 28th December 1889 and baptized there on 26th January 1890, lived in Harefield, enlisted in London on 11th February 1916. 24923, Private, 9th Royal Fusiliers (City of London Regiment), attached to the Manchester Regiment. Missing since 23rd July 1916, believed killed in action near Guillemont on that date or since, aged 26.

The war diary for the 9th Royal Fusiliers rather than the Manchester Regiment states that no casualties occurred on 23rd but at 1am on 24th the enemy continually shelled the front trenches at Mailly

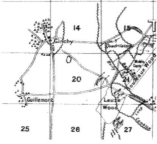

Ginchy, Bouleaux Wood and Leuze Wood

Maillet through the night and at 4pm a very heavy bombardment was put down on the 9th Royal Fusiliers communication trenches killing one man. Son of George and Mary Ann Tucker of The Plough, Hill End, Harefield. He was educated at Harefield School which he had joined from the infants' on 1st June 1897 and was a gardener to Mr. Billyard Leake at Harefield Park. He was a keen sportsman. On 26th September 1914, his grandmother, Elizabeth Thrift, who had lived in five reigns, had taken her first short ride in a car and was hoping to go out for a longer ride, but died on 22nd October 1914, aged 92. Cousin of George and Edward Ive who also died in the war. He is commemorated on Harefield War Memorial and on St. Marys' Church memorial. Commemorated: Thiepval Memorial, Somme, France.

TURVEY, Herbert
Born and lived at Harefield, enlisted at Hounslow on 12th August 1914. 1490, Private, 8th Royal Fusiliers. On 15th July 1915, the divisional front was extended to the south as far as due east of Armentieres, making a total distance of 7,000 yards. The 8th Royal

Fusiliers went into trenches at Houplines where they were greeted by the firing of 100 shells into the village in an hour. At about 11.30 on the morning of 18th August, he was in a working party building a new trench at Houplines close to the firing line when he was shot in the head and killed, aged 20. He suddenly gave a groan, stood upright and fell back flat on his back. Over 300 men were in this working party. Herbert was killed and another was wounded, both by the bullet from a rifle. Brother of Mrs. Ellen Saunders of 6 Newdigate Terrace, Harefield. He had worked for the British Portland Cement Company and had left with employees from Bell's United Asbestos and Osborne Stevens Co. He was born in August, enlisted in August and died in August. He is commemorated on Harefield War Memorial and the memorial at St. Mary's Church. Buried: Houplines Communal Cemetery Extension, Nord, A.3, France.

WALKER, Joseph

Born on 4th October 1896, son of John and Mary Ann Walker of 14 Waterloo Villas, High Street, Harefield. He had been educated at Harefield. 51426, Private, 13th Royal Fusiliers. Died on 25th November 1918, aged 23. He is commemorated on Harefield War Memorial and on St. Mary's Church memorial. Buried: Harefield (St. Mary) Churchyard.

WARD, C.

He is commemorated on Harefield War Memorial and on the Church Memorial. No C. Ward is listed on the SSFA document as having enlisted in the Army of the Navy prior to about the beginning of 1916.

WARD, J.
He is commemorated on the Bell's United Asbestos War Memorial. Possibly John Ward below.

WARD, John William

Born Nassington, Northants, enlisted Watford, of Harefield. 32179, Private, 2nd Bedfordshire Regiment. In the Savy sector on 22nd March 1918, the enemy entered the front line of the Battle Zone only to be driven back into Savy. At 2pm they again attacked and captured the whole front line. The 5th Army garrison, after making six local counter-attacks, fell back on 'Stevens Redoubt', the HQ's of the 2nd Bedfords, in the rear portion of the Battle Zone north of Etreillers. Just as the ammunition began to fail, orders were received from brigade HQs for a retirement on Ham, on the Somme. This withdrawal of the Bedfords from contact with the enemy was only accomplished at considerable cost. The 30th Division had held on to its ground until 4 in the afternoon. He was killed in action in France on 23rd March 1918, during the German spring offensive at St. Quentin. It was a disastrous day as the passage over the Somme at Peronne and the whole line of that river with it, was lost and there now lay no natural barrier to thwart the enemy's path to Amiens. Commemorated: Pozieres Memorial, Somme, France.

WARREN, Frederick
Born Saunderton, Bucks., enlisted Mill Hill, of Harefield. G/2513 (25313), Private, 2nd Middlesex Regiment. On first day of the Battle of the Somme,

1st July 1916, they were in action near Ovillers. After days of marching and entraining for different places, on 20th October they marched to Trones Wood and on 22nd were in the front line (Spectrum Trench). He was reported as killed in action in here in France at the Battle of Ancre Heights on 22nd October 1916. However, the war dairy records that there was nothing untoward on 22nd but on 23rd whilst in the trenches a total of 65 officers and men were killed, 117 men wounded and 47 men missing. The attack had begun at 2.30pm. He is not commemorated locally. Commemorated: Thiepval Memorial, Somme, France.

WATKINS, Charles Edward
Born on 25th March 1896, son of Alfred and Elizabeth Watkins of Highway Farm, Harefield. Enlisted at Shirehampton, of Highway Farm, Harefield. 210041, Bombardier, 158th Brigade, Royal Horse and Royal Field Artillery. Died of wounds in France on 31st May 1918, aged 22. A Canadian chaplain wrote that he had been 'sent back for a rest but must have returned to the firing line the same night as he was taken unconscious to a Canadian hospital on the 31st and died later the same day'. Educated at Harefield schools, after which he had worked on his father's farm at West Hyde. He joined the Remount Department at Shirehampton in February 1915, transferring in 1917 to the RFA at Woolwich. His father died on 28th October 1932, aged 62; his mother on 18th September 1944, aged 79. Buried: Pernes British Cemetery, Pas de Calais, E.10, France.

WATKINS, E. He is commemorated on Harefield War Memorial and on the Church Memorial. Maybe a mistake for Charles Edward Watkins.

WIGGINS, Benjamin
Born at Yiewsley on 2nd or 4th January 1897, son of Benjamin and Rose, and baptized at Yiewsley with his sister Edith on 28th January 1900, enlisted Uxbridge in 1912, resided at 2 Waterloo Villas, High Street, Harefield. T.F. 1884, Private, 1/8th Middlesex Regiment. Killed in action near Ypres in nerve-shaking sniping and bombing on or since 26th April 1915. On 23rd April 1915, 'D' Coy were on post duty north-west of Ypres. On 24th April 1915, 'D' Coy had already sent ammunition up the firing line for the Suffolk Regiment, and had joined the 3rd Royal Fusiliers as part of a digging party. They then went to Zonnebeke Dumping Ground. As night fell on Saturday 24th April 1915, the 1/8th Middlesex with their Division (28th) held their original trenches facing eastwards, south of St. Julien, preparing for an attack to be made at 6.30 on the following morning. They had been ordered to take up defensive positions where the enemy had broken the line held by the Canadians and the Cheshires. While the British were endeavouring to advance to the north, the Germans suddenly attacked the trenches held by the 28th Division, but were vigorously repulsed. He was reported missing, believed killed in action near Zonnebeke in the Battle of St. Julien on 26th April 1915, aged 25. Part of the German 27th Reserve Corps fell upon the 85th Brigade holding the line from Gravenstafel to Broodseinde. After bombarding the British front line with shrapnel, high explosives and gas-shells all morning, German infantry swarmed

across No-Man's Land and managed at several places to penetrate the defence of the front-line trenches, A hand-to-hand struggle followed. He was killed in action near Ypres at the Battle of St. Julien on 26th April 1915. All around were the dead and wounded. He had been reported as missing and his name appeared on a list from the German authorities received through the American Embassy that he had fallen and buried in the cemetery at Ehrenfriedhof, near Poelcapelle. He was educated at Harefield schools. He is commemorated on the War Memorial and at St. Mary's Church. After the Armistice he was reburied in the newly made Poelcapelle British Cemetery, Langemark-Poelkapelle, Belgium.

WIGGINS, Joseph Thomas
Born at Harefield on 4th July 1893, son of Joseph Thomas Wiggins and his wife Edith, and lived at Harefield, enlisted Marylebone. 17782, Corporal, 2nd Royal Berkshire Regiment. On 11th October 1918, the 8th Division was in action in an attack north of Vitry-en-Artois, delivered just before dawn. The enemy was holding the far bank of the Scarpe deviation in force. There were some troublesome machine-guns on the west bank which shelled our positions ceaselessly. In this action he was killed in action in France, during the final advance in Artois on 14th October 1918 when the 2nd Berks were attacking and pursuing the enemy. The forward area was heavily shelled from 3 – 7 pm by guns of every calibre and low levels of the front were subjected to gas shells. On the following day one ordinary rank was killed and 2 injured when a shell landed in the billet occupied by 'B' Coy. Meanwhile the British had launched a gas attack on German positions near

Ypres and it was on this day (14th October) that the 1st Company of the 16th Reserve Battalion of the Bavarian Infantry south of Ypres were subjected to this gas attack in which Private Adolf Hitler was temporarily blinded and taken by hospital train to a military hospital at Pasewalk in Pomerania. Joseph was educated at Harefield Schools. In late 1917 by chance he met his brother Billy of the Middlesex Regiment at the front. It had been so muddy that the enemy had become stuck in the mud. Sapper Wiggins went out with his platoon to search for them and while hunting spotted his brother coming home from a working party. Joseph, who may have joined the Royal Fusiliers at the start of the war,   is commemorated on the Bell's United Asbestos War Memorial as well as on both the village memorial and the Church memorial.   Cousin of Philip, below. Joseph's elderly father, foreman to the British Portland Cement Company at Harefield, was knocked down by a cyclist on the evening of 9th November 1921 as he was walking up Church Hill and died days later. Evidence of identification was given by Philip, one of his sons.   Commemorated: Vis-en-Artois Memorial, Pas de Calais, France.

WIGGINS, Phillip
Born Harefield on 3rd October 1893, enlisted at Charing Cross, Middx., in early December 1914, of Uxbridge. 59440, Sapper, Corps of Royal Engineers (73rd Field Coy., R. E.). In July 1915, the 73rd and 74th Field Companies moved to France. In preparation for an attack at Arras in April 1917, a section of the 73rd Field Company with the leading battalions from the 15th (Scottish) Division were sent for consolidation work. He was killed in action on

23rd April 1917, aged 23. On that date, our second general attack at Arras had taken place all along the nine-mile long line, but the German defences proved themselves and troops, especially those in the front line, were subjected to violent counter-attacks. Son of Mr. and Mrs. Phillip Wiggins of High Street, Harefield and cousin of Joseph. He was educated at Harefield schools. He is commemorated on Harefield War Memorial and the memorial at St. Mary's Church. Commemorated: Arras Memorial, Pas de Calais, France.

WINWRIGHT, G.

He is commemorated on the Bell's United Asbestos War Memorial. A Herbert Winwright (who had a brother named George) of 2 May Cottages, West Hyde who had served in the Boer War, was missing, believed killed in action on or about 1st August 1917 in the fighting at Westhoek. He was serving with the 'Queen's' (11th Royal West Surrey Regiment) and had worked at Bell's United Asbestos, where he played for their football team. He is commemorated on the Menin Gate Memorial at Ypres.

WOOD, William Henry

Born Bury St. Edmunds (or Bournemouth), of Harefield, joined up in September 1914. G/7090, Lance-Corporal, 4th Royal Fusiliers. Died in hospital of wounds to the abdomen on 12th October 1915, aged 23. From about 1st October 1915 until 17th October, the 4th Royal Fusiliers had been in Zouave Wood, where on most days shelling took place. Son of John and Florence Wood of 6 Fornham Road, Bury St. Edmunds. He had been employed at Harefield House as footman. He is not commemorated locally. Buried: Lijssenthoek Military Cemetery, Belgium.

WOODWARD, John

 Born Rickmansworth, lived and enlisted at Harefield. 28442, Sergeant, 4th Bedfordshire Regiment. Killed in action at Ourton in the Third Battle of Ypres on 30th October 1917 in the renewed attack on Passchendaele, after Sir Douglas Haig had ordered another short advance between the Roulers railway and the Westroosebeek road. In this renewed attack, which commenced at 5.50am they had found it very difficult to get forward on that day because of the heavy and boggy ground surrounding the Paddebeek. He is commemorated on the Bell's United Asbestos War Memorial, on Harefield War Memorial, at St Mary's Church at Harefield and also on the memorial at St. Mary's Church, Rickmansworth. Commemorated: Tyne Cot Memorial, Zonnebeke, West Vlaanderen, Belgium.

WYATT, James William

Born Shoreditch, Middx., enlisted Shoreditch, lived at Harefield. S/4474, Rifleman. 13th Rifle Brigade. Killed in action in France near Mametz Wood on 7th August 1916. Although there had been no important operations on this date, during the night shelling between 1.30am and about 7pm had caused many casualties. He was probably buried close to where he fell and his body reburied after the Armistice. Buried: Flatiron Copse Cemetery, Mametz, Somme, France.

YOUNG, Ernest Edwin

Born Harefield on about 6th October 1879 and  baptized there on November 30th 1879, son of Edwin and Lydia Lee Young, enlisted at Portsmouth, of Southampton. 31902, Private, 6th Wiltshire Regiment. Killed in action on 20th September 1917 in furious fighting near Polygon Wood, aged 38. Here they had captured and held a position in front of Hollebeke Chateau, at the Battle of Menin Road, part of the Third Battle of Ypres. The 19th Division captured two important woods- Bulgar and Belgian to form a firm flank in front of the village of Zandvoorde. Their course was down the spur east of Zillebeke and then into the small woods north of the Ypres-Comines Canal. By 9 o'clock the whole Klein Zillebeke sector had been made good. All actions in the northern sector of the battlefield on that date were subsidiary to the operations undertaken south of the Zonnebeke road, the aim being to engage the enemy between Langemarck and Zonnebeke in order to occupy him all along the Passchendaele line and prevent him from concentrating men and arms entirely around the Menin road. Son of Edwin (who died on 6th September 1922, aged 68) and the late Mrs. Lydia Lee Young (who had died on 4th November 1915, aged 61) of Harefield Lane, Harefield; husband of Irene C. L. Young of 90 Polden Street, Bridgwater, Somerset. He is commemorated on Harefield St. Mary's Church War Memorial and on Harefield War Memorial. Commemorated: Tyne Cot Memorial, Zonnebeke, West Vlaanderen, Belgium.

YOUNG, W.
He is commemorated on the Bell's United Asbestos
War Memorial.

SELECT BIBLIOGRAPHY

In the writing of this book, a large number of Regimental Histories have been used, too many to list.

The Great War: the standard history of the all-Europe conflict, edited by H.W. Wilson. The Amalgamated Press Limited, various volumes 1916-1921

The Times History of the War. The Times 1914-1919

Harefield School Admissions Register

British Red Cross & Order of St. John Enquiry List of the Wounded and Missing (various dates). Imperial War Museum

Captain Austin Hale Woodbridge's trench diary 21st April – 21st August 1915.

Citations of the Distinguished Conduct Medal in the Great War 1914-1920. N.& M. Press, 2007

CLUTTERBUCK, L.A. The Bond of Sacrifice: a biographical record of British Officers who fell in the Great War. N. & M. Press, 2002

De RUVIGNY'S Roll of Honour. N and M Press, 2003

DOYLE, A.C. The British Campaigns in Europe 1914-1918. Geoffrey Bles, 1923

The Middlesex County Times (various dates)

MORGAN, D. Lest we forget 1939-1945: Uxbridge, Ickenham, Harefield. Don Morgan, 2004

Percy House Hospital, Isleworth 'notebook', c1916'

Royal Flying Corps Communiqués 1914-1918 (several authors and publishers)

Soldiers' and Sailors' Families Associations (Uxbridge Division of Middlesex) reports 1914-c1916.

The Times newspaper 1914-1919

Various Regimental and Divisional Histories, in particular the use of maps from the following:

-History of the 12th (Eastern) Division in the Great War, 1914-1918, edited by Major General Sir Arthur Scott. Nisbet and Co., 1923

- HEADLAM, Cuthbert. History of the Guards Division in the Great War 1915-1918, Volume 1. John Murray, 1924

-ATKINSON, C.T. The Seventh Division 1914-1918. John Murray, 1927

La Grande Guerre vecue-racontee-illustree par les combatants 1914-1918. Librarie Aristide Quillet, 1930

MOSER, Otto Von. Die Wurttemberger im Weltkrieg. Belagsbuchhandlung, 1927

Von Kluck, A. The march on Paris and the Battle of the Marne 1914. Edward Arnold, 1920